The Pragmatic

YOGESH PANDEY

Yogesh Pandey

First published in 2017 by

Becomeshakespeare.com
Wordit Content Design & Editing Services Pvt Ltd
Unit - 26, Building A-1, Nr Wadala RTO, Wadala (East),
Mumbai 400037, India
T:+91 8080226699

Copyright © 2017 by
All rights reserved. Any unauthorized reprint or use of this material is prohibited. No part of this book may be reproduced or transmitted in any form or by any means, electronic or mechanical, including photocopying, recording, or by any information storage and retrieval system without express written permission from the author/publisher.
Please do not participate in or encourage piracy of copyrighted materials in violation of the author's rights. Purchase only authorized editions.

©
ISBN: 978-93-86487-49-0

The Pragmatic

To

My dear siblings

For the noble deed of paying all my bills.
Aspiring to be an author, I thus assure you more such opportunities in the near future.

Yogesh Pandey

Acknowledgement

So there are these people who are so jobless that they care to read the page of acknowledgement. If you're among those, let me tell you, I really like you as I belong to that jobless class.

Writing is fun. Grammar isn't.

But grammar is that element which has potential to make your book unbearable to the lot who understand the notorious subject. Frankly, I don't. So, I would like to express my sincere gratitude to those who had the patience to read the early drafts of the manuscript, sometimes more than once, highlighting hundreds of edits. Prathamesh, Ziad and Hitesh, I will always be grateful for this. I would also like to thank Aniket and Sanket for their valuable inputs.

Everyone who has read the manuscript and has shared his/her feedback has a positive influence on this work. The list is too big to jot down here but if you're reading this, you know I am talking about you and I want you know that I am really thankful.

Love,
Yogesh.

The Pragmatic

Yogesh Pandey

1.

I opened my eyes and found myself in an alien environment. The horrifying darkness made it difficult to see anything around. My eyes slowly adjusted to the darkness as I gained back my consciousness. I discovered that I was lying naked in a room. I panicked. I screamed aloud, which I shouldn't have done. There was a wall in front of me and I could hear noises coming from the television set behind the wall. No sooner than I screamed that the television set was muted and I heard footsteps approaching towards the room I was in.

The door opened making a crinkling sound. A silhouette of a thin, tall man with curly hair appeared. I brought my knees close to my chest hiding my body. As I did, I felt pain in between my legs.

The man pressed a switch which switched on a tungsten bulb and lightened the room in yellow colour. He was now visible. He was wearing a shirt inner and old jeans which were torn up to the knees and few strands of threads were hanging from the bottom of his jeans. His face was dark, unpleasant and unbearably ugly to look at. He was holding a TV remote in his hand and was chewing beetle leaf which made his lips look hot red. He spat beetle juice in a dustbin, which was full of stains and walked towards me. He sat on the bed on which I was lying.

I was terribly scared.

'Don't be afraid,' he spoke and his breathe stank like a gutter,

The Pragmatic

'consider me as your friend.'

'What-did-you-do- to me-?'

'Nothing, I didn't even place a finger on you,' he said.

Then followed a brief pause.

'I didn't but someone else did,' he added with a wicked smile.

'Who?' I asked.

'I don't reveal my customer's identity. Business ethics, you know.'

'Please let me go,' I begged.

'I can't. It's too risky. Now your fate has brought you here. Stay here, soon you will adapt yourself. And believe me, given your sexy looks, one day you will become queen of this place.'

He sounded terrible. I was understanding what he meant, but I didn't want to accept it. I didn't want to accept that this was real. I didn't want to imagine myself as he was expecting me to.

'One more advice, cooperate till you adapt. It will be less painful for you,' he said and left.

He came again after a couple of minutes and threw some clothes in front of me. I didn't look at him.

'Wear it till we get something for you,' he said and left.

As soon as he left I took the stinky clothes, a lousy t-shirt and oversized shorts.

I looked around the place. The room was a very small one without *any window. There was a small table beside the bed on which I was lying. On the table there were many alcohol bottles, cigarette packets and a lighter. The room was coloured in red and the tungsten light reflecting off the red walls made it irritatingly bright.*

I was thinking of Baba. I was thinking of getting out of this place. I was hoping that somehow he will find me. I was not able to understand how much time had passed since they brought me here neither was I able to guess whether it was day or night.

I felt totally helpless.

I rested my back on the wall behind me and as I did I saw droplets of blood on the bed sheet. I buried my face in my knees and started to cry. Crying was the best feeling.

2.

'We seek the love we think we deserve.'

I was reading 'The perks of being a wallflower' by Stephen Chbosky and this line was just too abstract for my comprehension. I wondered what it meant but was unable to figure it out. Lost in my thoughts, I looked up at the Professor and gave her a nod pretending that I was paying attention and understood whatever she had just said. Meanwhile, a shadow entered the classroom followed by the girl casting it. In no time Kabir moved his elbow hitting it on my right shoulder.

'*Teri bhabhi aa gayi,*' he said.

In just three months she was the sixth girl he had called my *bhabhi*. His last crush had already blocked his both facebook accounts. But according to Kabir, she still had a soft corner for him.

'Bhabhi? She is too pretty to be your sister,' I said in a low voice.

'I know you are jealous of me,' he said pronouncing the word jealous like *jelly-us*. 'But I won't mind, you know, I have a kind heart. I forgive you.' I threw him a dirty look.

After a couple of minutes the professor said the most awaited words, 'we will see this in the next lecture,' and left. I poked Priya, who was sitting on the bench to my left, wondering whether she was planning to attend the next lecture. Kabir looked at me with the same suspicion.

We walked around the fountain, the one which never had any water flowing through it, near the main building walking towards the canteen. On the left side of the road was a small garden exactly in front of the main library. Many of the students prefer to sit in the garden holding their books with their eyes never making any contact with them. Increased testosterone level isn't good for concentration.

'Arijit, at your 9'o clock,' Kabir said pointing at a girl on my left side, 'eight'.

'Nah, she is not even a six,' I said. 'She looks like she has been decorated.'

'Pathetic!' Priya said. 'Who are you to rate them? I mean seriously look at yourselves. Morons.'

'You are *jelly-us* because we can talk among ourselves and also comment on one other's choices. But you cannot.' Kabir said.

'First thing, two people do things *between* them, not *among* them. Second, it should be *each other's choices* not *one another's choices*,' Priya said.

'Can you stop this? This, *unbearable-know-it-all*, attitude?' Kabir said.

'Sure I can, but obviously, I won't,' she replied and confused Kabir.

The Pragmatic

We reached the canteen. *Anna's* canteen, it was called. Like an old Bollywood movie, it featured old broken benches, lousy waiters with their untidy shirts half unbuttoned and an arrogant old man at the counter. The only reason we came here was besides being cheap, it offered refreshing tea. As we entered, Priya waved her hand at a girl sitting in the corner. She was the same girl Kabir had made my *bhabhi* couple of minutes earlier.

As we sat a man came holding a piece of cloth in his hand to clean the table. I looked at Kabir and said, 'one tea for me and a Ban-Wada for the pretty lady.'

'Fine,' he replied. 'But where is the pretty lady? Is your friend going to join us Priya?'

She kicked him under the table.

'You bitch,' he shouted.

She leaned forward and whispered, 'you asshole.'

'My turn,' I said, 'you rascals.'

'Two cups of tea and bring something poisoned for her,' Kabir said to the man who was absent-mindedly wiping our table. The man ignored Kabir and walked away. Priya laughed thunderously. I joined her. Then another boy with a serving plate in his hands approached our table.

'*Bhaiya do chai…*'

And he too left as soon as I opened my mouth. This time, it was Kabir's turn to laugh.

'You are overreacting,' I said. He then stopped shaking his body and laughed in a more human way.

'That's better.'

Finally, the same boy arrived to take our order.

'What's her name?' Kabir asked eyeing towards Priya's friend.

'Shefali,' Priya said looking at me with an evil expression on her face. Kabir was lost in Shefali.

'Shefali, what a beautiful name!' he said.

'And she is completely your type,' Priya said.

'His type? Is she having a dozen pairs of stinking socks hanging outside her room?' I asked. They ignored me.

Priya still carried her intense look.

'She was asking about you,' she said.

'Close your mouth first, Kabir,' I said. 'Priya, do you have her number, you can help our fellow friend.'

'No, I don't. But I can give Kabir's number to her and ask her to call him. In this way, Kabir won't seem too desperate.'

She was a good actor but it seemed that she had lost her mind. Kabir will definitely spot her lie, I thought.

'Will you do that for me?' Kabir asked as his eyes brightened up with hope. I gave him an *are you so stupid* look, which he ignored.

'Sure, I am your friend and besides I know you two will make a great couple,' she said.

'Priya, you are not just my friend, you are the best one I ever had,' Kabir said lifting his cup of tea and his eyes still fixed on Shefali.

I laid on my bed and held my phone impatiently, waiting for a reply. The door knocked with a continuous banging noise. It was Kabir and this was his style of knocking to annoy me.

'It's open,' I said. He pushed the door and entered dancing with his phone. He took the chair from under the study table, rotated it and sat with his oversized stomach resting on the back of the chair. He unlocked his phone and showed me a text message which I had sent him a couple of minutes earlier.

```
Hi kabir
dis is shefali. Priyas frnd.
```

Priya gave me her old sim card to tease Kabir. This was her plan. I was trapped in it as she was not well versed with texting language. In spite of the 160 alphabet-limit in text messaging services, she made it a point to spell every word correctly and expected me to do the same. When I didn't follow her rule, she wouldn't reply.

Kabir was on cloud nine.

'That sounds great,' I said pretending to be curious. 'What did you reply?'

'I haven't, yet.'

'Nervous?' I asked.

'No. Just got the message.'

'So what are you waiting for?' I asked.

'You are right, what am I waiting for...' he said to himself. He then took the phone from my hand and started to type.

'By the way, what are you going to say?'

'Obviously, that I like her.'

'Don't be so desperate. Have some patience. You hardly know her,' I said. 'What if she stops talking to you? Think twice before you say anything stupid.'

'Hmm you are right,' he nodded in agreement, 'but what shall I say then?'

'Ask about her, girls like to talk about themselves. Try to be a good listener.'

'Okay sir,' he erased what he had typed and started to think again. He looked up with an innocent smile and asked, 'but what should I ask?'

'Just say Hi.'

'Yeah, Hi sounds pretty decent,' he said smiling and looked back on his cell phone.

Meanwhile, I set my phone in silent mode. I got a message:

Hi ☺

I didn't respond to his text. He was getting impatient, started shaking his legs, checking his phone every ten seconds and pretending that he was just checking time. Ten minutes passed and Kabir hadn't spoken a word. Which was very unusual.

'I think she has not received my message. Shall I message her again?' he asked.

'She has received your message and she will reply soon. Have some patience.'

'She must be thinking I am not interested in her,' he said, 'I just said *Hi*, I should have added something more.'

'Like?'

'I don't know, maybe that I like her.'

'Shut up and let's go eat, I am starving,' I said as I stood up. 'She might be having her dinner and so she isn't replying.'

'Hopefully,' he said in a hopeless voice, 'you carry on. I am not coming to mess, I will have some snacks later on,' he said and stood up to leave.

'Okay, as you wish,' I said locking the door. Kabir went directly to his room without snooping into anyone else's room. Which was again very unusual for him.

I took out the phone as I walked and typed a message:

Sry for late rply. Was havng dinr.

I was both amused and worried as I pressed the *send* button. I typed another message:

He seems 2 b very serious.

I sent it to Priya.

Then I realised my mistake. I typed another message:

He seems to be very serious.

My cell beeped, it was Priya.

LOL :P

'2' instead of 'to' and 'b' instead of 'be' was not allowed. 'LOL' was allowed. Cheater.

———

I placed my phone on the table. Asked for some *Chapatis*. Unwillingly, poured some capsicum on my plate. Monotonously, I started to eat.

'Arijit,' someone poked me.

I looked back and saw Kabir taking the seat next to me. In his right hand he held his phone like the most precious thing in the world. He showed me the screen placing it just a few millimetres away from my face.

'Take a look, *teri bhabhi ka message he*,' he said.

'The screen is blank,' I said and the boys sitting on the opposite side of the table started giggling.

'Whoops!' he said and unlocked his phone. Then he turned the phone's screen towards me. This time at a visible distance.

'See, I told you,' I said. This was so far my favourite phrase. 'Have some patience.'

'Stop saying that and tell me what to say next.'

'Nothing, Let her wait for a while.'

'No. Waiting is not good. Besides, why should I make her wait unnecessarily?'

The Pragmatic

'If you want to listen then wait. Or else tell her that you like her and spoil everything.'

'Okay-okay,' he said and put his phone inside his breast pocket and started to eat unmindfully.

He passed his curd to me. I took it. Typed another message with my free hand and pressed the send button.

Seems dat u r busy.
Sry 2 distrb.
Babye.

'Whom are you talking to?' he asked me.

'Uh, Priya,' I said.

He took out his phone as soon as it beeped. He gave me an angry look. 'Let her wait, *asshole*,' he mumbled to himself. 'Now, I won't listen to you. Let me handle this on my own.'

'What are you talking about? Is it her message?' I asked.

'Nothing. Eat your food,' he said staring at the screen and began typing.

'Okay, as you say,' I said.

I received a message from him.

No dear no busy 4 u

I replied:

Cho chweet of you ☺

Kabir: Thnku ☺
  so whats up

Shefali: nthng just chatting.

Kabir's face turned pale.

Kabir: wid?

Shefali: wid u fool :p

He smiled coyly. I asked why he was smiling. He said it was none of my business.

Kabir: u luk pretty in pink

Shefali: Thnku ☺ U look cul in red.

Kabir started blushing. He showed me the message and gave a proud smile. I faked a teasing smile.

Kabir: Thnku sooo much. I'll wear red 2mrw again

I laughed reading the message. Kabir gave me a suspicious look. I remained silent. He asked what happened.

'Nothing, it's just Priya asking me to type correct spellings.'

'Oh,' he said still looking suspicious.

I thought to be more careful next time.

Shefali: cul.

Kabir: Can I ask u smthng??

Shefali: wat?

Kabir: do u hav any bf??

Shefali: bf? Matlab?

Kabir: do u hav any boyfrnd?

Shefali: no.

Kabir: even I don hav any bf :P

I washed my hands quickly, wiped them and checked my inbox gesturing Kabir that I would be waiting outside. The message read:

Hahaha!!

Shefali: did u hav any bf earlier?

Kabir: no....no I m an innocent boy.

Shefali: I was kiddin innocent boy :p

'Arijit, what do you mean by *kiddin*?' Kabir came out.

'What she meant is she was kidding, as in teasing.'

'Okay, then it's fine,' he said 'but how do you know it's she, not he?'

'It's written on your face,' I said and made a mental note to be careful next time.

3.

Slothfully, I took my phone in my hand. There were two options. *Confirm* and *snooze*. I selected the snooze option, covered my face with the blanket and tried to sleep again thinking about what I just dreamed. I woke up after three more snoozes. Pushed the blanket away with my legs. Checked my inbox and saw five new messages from Kabir. I put the phone back on the table.

I pulled my bucket from under the table. Put all the bathing and brushing stuff inside it. Locked the room and walked towards room no. 186. I knocked very hard for some time. A huge figure opened the door. I entered and he went back into his blanket.

'Kabir,' I shouted.

'Hmm,' he replied.

'Get up,' I said in a lazy voice.

'Hmm,' he replied.

'C'mon I am not going to wait for you again,' I said.

'Hmm,' he replied.

'Okay, I am leaving then,' I said.

'Hmm,' he replied.

I stood up and turned.

'Arijit,' he said in a dizzy voice.

'What?'

'I am suffering from the disease that Priya told us about. The one in which it gets difficult to get out of your bed.'

'It isn't a disease. What she mentioned was Dysania,' I said.

'Whatever, the point is I am not lazy, it is just D-y-s-a-n-i-a,' he said smiling, 'and one more thing.'

'What?'

'I was wondering,' he said still in a dizzy voice, 'if we aren't allowed to use ceiling fans in our rooms then what are these iron hooks for?'

'In case if you wish to commit suicide,' I said.

'Why would I commit suicide?'

'Let me think, hmm, maybe because Shefali already got a boyfriend.' I said sitting on the chair again.

'No, she did not,' he said taking out his bucket.

'How are you so sure about it?' I asked.

'She told me,' he said.

'Oh so things are speeding up,' I said, 'but how do you know she was not lying?'

'Why would she lie to me?' Kabir asked.

'Why wouldn't she? You barely know her.'

'But then why did she ask Priya about me?' Kabir asked.

'How would I know?' I asked and signalled him to get out of the room. 'Maybe she found you cute. I mean like *puppy cute.*'

Kabir's face turned pale.

———

We rested on the porch surrounding a tree near the Mathematics department. As usual, we were late for the first lecture. Priya had probably arrived in time. I was texting her to ask where she was. Suddenly, Kabir started moving his ankle back and forth hurting my abdomen. I turned towards him. He seemed uncomfortable and was eyeing me to look at my backside. Shefali was approaching us.

'What should I do? What should I say?' Kabir asked staring at her.

'For starters, stop staring at her,' I said.

She came nearer. Kabir became nervous. She turned right and went straight to the department.

'What should you say to her? Bye!' I said.

'Very funny,' he replied.

'You were very nervous, weren't you? I asked.

'Of course, I was. This is my first time you know…' Kabir said and I interrupted.

'First time! You liar, you bloody liar,' I said. 'What about Palakh and Aarti and Nitu and Radhika and what was her name, the latest one…'

'They are my past. This is my future. Can you please let me focus?'

'At present, it seems that your future is not recognizing you. Which creates a strong possibility of her being in your past list in a while.'

'No way. I think she is too shy to start a conversation on her own. I must take the initiative.'

'Sure, you must,' I said patting his back, 'let's go right now.' I stood up.

'But what shall I say?'

'You decide. Move fast before she enters the classroom.'

'Don't hurry. I can talk with her after the class.'

'Okay, as you say. For now, let's go to the class then.'

We moved towards the class. Most of our fellow classmates were walking in the opposite direction. I saw Priya amongst them.

She waved at us. We walked towards her and she informed us that the lecture was off as the professor was out of station. We started walking downstairs. Kabir walked behind us. I briefed Priya about Shefali's scenario warning her that if anything went wrong she was solely responsible. She nodded.

'Kabir, did Shefali call you yesterday? I gave her your number,' Priya asked as we sat on the same porch.

'She sent a text message saying *hi* and we conversed for a while after that,' Kabir said. He was carefully scanning the mob of students passing in front of us.

'That sounds good,' Priya said. 'So what you guys talked about? Did she tell you about her boyfriend, Manoj?'

'What?' Kabir shouted.

'Calm down, I am just kidding,' Priya said and laughed.

'Funny,' Kabir said sarcastically.

'Anyway the important thing is,' Priya said looking at me, 'I am not going to sign any more proxies for you two fools. I almost got caught today.'

'Priya, did I tell you how beautiful you look today in this blue dress?' I said.

'That's not going to work,' she said.

'And your white dupatta, it's just too cute,' Kabir said.

'And the Warli painting on your bangles shows your love and respect for ancient art,' I said.

'And those loafers remind me of my grandmother's bathroom chappals,' Kabir said.

We both looked at Kabir and he muttered, 'whoops!'

'I told you that's not going to work,' Priya said.

'Let's make a deal then,' Kabir was serious now. 'You will sign our proxy, okay?'

'And?' Priya asked.

'And nothing. That's it. You will sign our proxies. That's the deal.'

'Shut up,' Priya said.

I took out my cell phone and typed a message.

Kabir's cell beeped. He checked the message and hiding it from Priya he showed it to me. The message was:

Din u recognize me? I passd in front f u fw min ago

Then he began typing.

'Which is next?' I asked Priya.

'Don't know, may be Algebra, I guess. Can I see your cell for a minute?'

'You shouldn't check a boy's phone. You may regret it later,' I said.

Kabir started to laugh, 'imagine her checking my phone.'

'Take this,' I gave my phone still laughing. 'At your own risk,' I added.

She took my phone with the tips of her finger touching mine. It was a pleasant touch. I wondered whether she too found it pleasant. I wondered whether she even noticed it. I wondered why I was wondering so much.

She started to laugh reading more than a hundred messages Shefali and Kabir had exchanged yesterday.

'What are you laughing at?' Kabir asked, still typing.

'Nothing, Arijit got some good collection of funny memes in here.'

My phone beeped. It was surely Kabir. Priya checked the message.

'Hey you are not supposed to check my messages,' I said. I placed my open palm in front of her asking to have my phone back.

'Is there something you think you can hide from me?'

'Yes there are many things you don't know about me' I said.

'Like?'

'Like…you don't know…about… ahem,' I said, 'well I quit.' There were a lot of things I could have said but I liked the feeling that she thought she knew everything about me.

She checked Kabir's message and faced the screen towards my side, still having an evil smile on her face.

I thght u din recgnize me. Hw stupid v r :P

I wondered what the evil smile on her face meant. But pretty soon I got my answer. Kabir showed me another message and left alone towards canteen. The message was:

I m at d cantn. Can u cum here?

'Hey, where are you going?' Priya asked.

'Arijit will tell you. See you guys after the next lecture.'

'What if Shefali is there at the IMDR canteen?' I asked Priya.

'Priyanka. Her name is Priyanka. And yes, she is there,' she said.

'What? Have you gone crazy?' I asked.

'Calm down and enjoy. Stop being so *fattoo*,' she said.

It hurts when your crush calls you a *fattoo*. I kept quiet and thought of calling Kabir and telling him the truth. I should've done that but after being called a coward this was the last thing I would've done.

Priya stood up and lifted her bag. 'You are coming for the lecture, aren't you?'

'Oh yeah. Let's go,' I said still thinking to call Kabir back.

4.

Boring would have been a compliment for that lecture. We sat on the third bench of the first row from the left door. The Professor was writing something on the board which seemed not so difficult but at the same time not worth my attention, especially, when I was sharing my desk with Priya. I liked the times when Kabir was not in the lecture with us.

'I yam goinga to conduk next pryactical in dhis lekchar as I yam nat there today yin the afternoon.'

'I am going to conduct next practical in this lecture as I am not there today in the afternoon,' Prof Iyer said in his thick south Indian accent.

As usual, I turned towards Priya begging again to give me one more practical sheet. After I begged enough she gave me one. We copied the questions written on the board and watched some intelligent beings solve them. On the other hand, we waited for Prof Iyer to write the answers in the end. Meanwhile, I asked Priya to continue with our word association game.

'Okay, but where were we?' She asked.

'I don't remember,' I said, 'let's start over again, you first.'

'Okay,' she said, 'Algebra.'

'Seriously, you want to start with Algebra?' I asked.

The Pragmatic

'Stop complaining and start playing,' she said.

'Okay then, ah...Prof Iyer.'

'Boredom.'

'Electronics.'

'Circuit.'

'Circuit diagrams.'

'Complex.'

'You.'

'Complex? Me? What the hell?' she said loud enough to get professor's attention.

He gave us an intense look. He didn't say a word but with his firm gaze asked us to maintain silence. Those dark eyes were capable of provoking terror.

'Stop complaining,' I wrote on the last page of my notebook and slid it on her side.

'Journalist,' she wrote.

'News.'

'Television.'

'TV series.'

'F.R.I.E.N.D.S.'

'Characters.'

'Phoebe.'

'Weird.'

'You.'

That was her revenge for *Complex-you.*

'And now suddenly I am weird?' I asked. I was louder than I should have been. The class fell unusually silent. I hoped that we were not the reason behind the silence. We looked up. Professor stared at us and threw a horrifying expression. He made a gesture with his hands asking us to stand up. We did. Our eyes fixed on the floor.

'*Lasta warninga, wonna more time and you are outa.*'

'Last warning, one more time and you are out,' he said. We nodded, still looking at the floor.

'*Keepa standing.*'

'Keep standing,' he said and turned his back towards us. We sighed.

I was feeling embarrassed standing in the class. I looked at Priya who was laughing.

'Stop laughing,' I wrote in the notebook.

'Let's continue,' she whispered slowly.

'Gone crazy? I have no intentions of going out of the class,' I said.

She took the book and wrote *fattoo* in it.

'Sexy.'

'Attitude.'

'Personality.'

'Beauty.'

'Kate Winslet.'

'Titanic.'

'Painting.'

She looked at me for a while then she wrote:

'Romance.'

From the corner of her eye she tried to look while I was writing.

'You,' I wrote and could feel her eyes moving from the book towards me. I ignored her and completed my word by adding *th* so it became *youth* and passed the book to her.

She laughed.

'Us.'

Now, what was I supposed to write after that? I thought for a while. Nothing was popping up in my mind. I was forcing myself to come up with something and escape this awkward moment. But nothing came up.

'Standing,' I wrote eventually. Overthinking's a bitch.

She gave an *ew* expression. I shrugged my shoulders.

'Standing ovation.'

'Respect.'

'Woman,' she said instead of writing.

Our eyes were fixed on the floor again and Professor was scolding us. This time, his temper was very high. He came near our bench and asked us to show whatever we had written. We showed him the questions we wrote.

'Where are the answers?' he asked pronouncing each word correctly. I looked at him and wondered whether he noticed that he pronounced each word correctly.

'We tried but…,' Priya said but wasn't allowed to continue.

'Where dida youve triya? showu me'

'Where did you try? Show me,' he said.

Both of us looked down again. He took our practical sheets and tore them into pieces. I wanted him to know that I begged hard to get the sheet. But I kept quiet.

'Getta out, nowu'

'Get out, now,' he shouted.

Normally we would have apologized promising that it won't happen again. But he was too furious to listen anything from our end. We kept quiet and left. Once we were at a safe distance from the class we started to laugh loudly. I called Kabir to check what happened with Shefali.

We met him near the same tree. He was looking little upset.

'I went to the IMDR canteen. She was sitting with her friends. So I took the table next to theirs and sat facing her back,' Kabir said.

'I texted her that I had reached and we can talk when she is done with her friends.'

'And?' Priya asked curiously.

The Pragmatic

'After some time she left with her friends, I even called her name but she ignored. She didn't even reply to my text,' he said in a sad voice.

Of course, she will ignore if you call her with this name, I thought and wondered why I haven't received his message.

'She is a girl. We need some time to trust anyone in such matters,' Priya said.

'She might have changed her mind after looking you properly,' I added.

'Can you please shut up for a while?' he said.

'She is not showing any interest in you, why the hell you are getting mad at me?' I said.

'True. But you are not supposed to make fun of my sentiments. You better remember this.'

'Surely, I will,' I said.

'Anyway, I am running out of balance can I use your phone to make a call. It's urgent.'

'Sure,' I said.

5.

The door opened again. My heart started pounding heavily. He came back with another guy of similar physique just a little shorter than him. The other guy looked at me with an indecent expression and murmured something in his ears. Both of them laughed. I was horrified.

'I have been very gentle with you so far,' he said with a terror in his voice, 'but now it is business time. Do whatever the man will ask for. Cooperate and things will be much easier for everyone and less painful for you.'

I was still sitting with my knees close to my chest and was weeping. His words made me shiver.

'Please, please let me go, I'll give you anything you want but for God's sake let me go,' I begged.

'Every woman is the same,' the short guy said.

'Just wait for few months baby. Then you will never want to leave our world and go back to the world of yours. I have witnessed this with many other chicks,' he said.

Both of them left and locked the door from outside. They turned off the lights before leaving. I was shivering very hard. The room around me was completely dark. My eyes were so adapted to the darkness that they would have hurt if exposed to daylight. I had no idea what time it was or whether it was day or night. I was wondering why everyone was taking so long to find me. I had started doubting whether I would be able to meet them again, whether I would be able to see the outside world again.

After around ten minutes the door crinkled again. He entered and was looking back towards someone.

'Come saheb, come,' he said as a silhouette of another man followed him. He switched on the dark yellow light. After being in darkness for so long the light was very painful. That is what he meant when he said that after a while women do not wish to leave this place. Like my eyes, I too will adapt to this darkness and after that living in light would be more painful.

I lifted my arm to block the light and watched the man approaching me.

He was a fair old man in his early fifties. He was moderately fat and wore a shiny blue velvet shirt and a khakhee coloured trousers. He carried a very expensive watch in one hand and a golden bracelet in the other. He was half bald and had blood red eyes. A mark of a scar stretched from left of his nose to his right eye.

'You are sure you will be able to handle her? She is a new piece,'

'Sure. Rebel gives me more pleasure,' he said staring towards me.

The thin boy left and locked the door from outside. The man had an alcohol bottle in his hand. He took a sip and placed the bottle on the table. He then removed his bracelet and watch and sat on my bed.

'Don't be scared,' he said gently, 'you are my daughter's age. I won't cause you any harm. Cooperate and it will be easier for both of us.'

REBEL GIVES ME PLEASURE, was all I heard.

His words were echoing in my ears. He started unbuttoning his shirt.

'No, no, please don't do this. Please let me go. Please. I beg you,' I cried.

'Surrender yourself to me and you will be pleased. If you don't, it won't be very pleasing to you,' he said as he removed his arms from his shirt and threw the shirt on the ground. He bent and crawled towards me.

I glued myself to the corner. I was sobbing. He tried to climb over me I pushed him away with my legs.

'So you choose the painful option. Good,' he said and again moved towards me, this time very ferociously. He grabbed my little biceps with his rough hands and brought his face close to my breasts.

I panicked. I again tried to push him away and kicked in between his legs. His grip on my biceps lightened and he moved away cursing.

'You bloody whore, you have to pay for this,' he said and he fell on the ground.

Slowly he stood up, went to the door and knocked. The thin boy opened the door. He went out.

The thin boy and the short boy came inside. The short one was having a rope in his hand. I was horrified. He grabbed my legs and the thin one grabbed my hands. They both stretched me straight on the bed. The thin boy slapped me on my face.

'So you think you are strong? I warned you earlier- If you cooperate it would be less painful. Now you will see what I meant.'

He tied both my hands to the upper edge of the bed. The short guy who was sitting on my legs forced my pant out. I tried moving my legs to push him away but he was sitting on my knees which made it difficult to move my legs. He then undressed himself, stood on his knees, lifted my legs on his shoulders and forced him inside me.

I screamed.

First with rage, anger, rebel. Then with pain, helplessness, fear. At last, I surrendered myself. I was not feeling anything anymore. I did nothing.

After some time the short boy was done. He moved away.

Now the thin boy came. It was his turn.

After they both were done, they sent the fat man inside. It was his turn.

6.

It was a lazy Sunday morning. My watch showed 11 am and I was still lying on my bed inside my blanket, replying to Kabir's nonstop messages. It was fun flirting with Kabir. He accepts any reason I, Shefali, gave for any strange behaviour like the one which happened at the IMDR canteen. He gave replies to any message within seconds, except for a few times when he came to my room asking me to translate whatever he had in his mind.

When Shefali asked him to wear his same red shirt every day for past five days, he agreed. She said that she feels shy talking to him in person and hence will only talk through chat. He agreed. She said that at her home she is not allowed to talk to boys on the phone and so they can't talk on the phone. He agreed. I was enjoying it and so was he. Both of us unaware of the trouble that was about to come.

Kabir came to my room and we chatted for a while.

'Are you sure?' I asked feeling uneasy.

'Yes, sure than anything else,' he said. His face turned scarlet.

Kabir said that he wanted to ask Shefali out for a date. What made me worried was the determination with which he said that. I left the room saying that I needed to go to the washroom. I was thinking that I should tell him that Shefali doesn't exist and it was me. But I was afraid of the consequences. I also wanted to say that it was Priya's plan and I resisted. I entered my room again realising that it was too late to have any of these arguments. Kabir was holding my phone in one hand and his own in the other hand. He called Shefali and found that my phone started ringing with his name before the *calling* suffix.

He placed my cell on the table and about to leave when he saw me at the door. He came closer, gave me a vaguely blank look and left. I didn't have the courage to follow him.

I sat on my bed thinking about what could be done next. I called Priya but her phone was switched off. I called her mother and she was attending some friend's marriage.

Finally, I took a deep breath and went to his room. I knocked but he didn't respond.

'He is not in his room,' I said. I briefed Priya about the scenario and got scolded for leaving my phone with Kabir.

'Did you try calling him?' Priya asked still in a casual tone.

'I am calling him for more than an hour,' I said 'He is not answering my call.'

'Wait I will try to call him. Till then you take a look around the hostel. He must be in one of the rooms.'

'Okay,' I said and hung up the phone.

'No response. Did you find him anywhere?' Priya asked.

'No, I searched the campus. Few of the fellow hostel mates are helping me but I think he is not in the campus,' I said.

'I will be there in half an hour, you keep looking for him,' she said and hung the phone.

―――

'Any news?' she asked in an impatient manner as she walked towards me.

'Nothing,' I said, 'I told you…'

'Yes, I know you told me earlier that we should not play this prank. You were right. Happy?' she said, 'now, tell me, did you check the hill?'

'No, my friends did, but I don't trust them. I think he could be there.'

'Let's go then,' she said and we left.

I sent a text to Kabir.

It was a hot sunny day and I was in no mood of climbing the hill. I was regretting agreeing to the idea of going on the hill

'Can't you walk faster?' She said.

I tried to walk a bit faster but was too tired to do so. Damn Kabir, it was his plan to call her at the hill.

We walked along the contours, passing through the cemented water tanks we reached near the temple. I sat on the water storage tank. Priya was running around the temple, checking every corner. She walked down the path, disappeared for a while and then turned up running towards other direction and repeated the same process in every possible direction.

'Kabir-Kabir,' Priya shouted.

'Kabir-Kabir,' I joined her just for the sake of not putting up an impression that I was of no use.

'I think he must be lying under the shade of the tower,' Priya said moving quickly in the direction of the tower.

It wasn't a tower in any sense. But we don't know what it was, so we called it a tower. I sat on the cement base of the tower and rested back on one of the pillars. Priya again started running up and down looking for him. I glanced around the inner portion of the tower and listened to Priya shouting Kabir's name from a far distance.

'Move, you moron,' she shouted returning from one of her down trips. 'Check there,' she pointed towards my back. I was glad that she sent me in a direction I didn't want her to go. I turned back, took few steps in slow motion and then looked back at her. She was standing with both her hands on her waist looking aggressively towards me.

'Move faster,' she shouted and I immediately went down a few steps, enough to disappear from her sight. I heard her footsteps fading. I climbed back taking a piece of paper from my pocket put some dust over it and shouted 'Priya, I found something.'

She came back rested her hands on her knees bending through her waist, 'what?'

'Here's a letter addressed to us. I found it under the stone behind this pillar.'

I handed the dust covered letter to Priya. It was Kabir's handwriting. She unfolded the letter:

To,
Arijit and Priya,

I know you will come searching me here. Hopefully, you will find this letter soon.

I know I am little stupid and sentimental but that doesn't mean that my best friends are supposed to make fun of it. I was thinking very seriously about Shefali, trying to present myself in an honest manner not knowing that I was talking to Arijit and entertaining both of you. The day before yesterday, I downloaded her photograph from facebook and sent it to my mother. She approved, giving me permission to ask her out for a date.

Today she will ask me what happened, tell me what I should say? That her son is dumb? That his best friends were enjoying making fun of his feelings? You guys don't know what she thinks of me.

You have no idea that how I will feel facing both of you. And if you have involved others, which most probably you had already done, I won't be able to face them as well. Both of you are smart and people always treat you in a decent manner but you will never realize how it feels when people treat you as a jerk, not to mention when these people are your best friends. At least according to me you were.

I don't want to talk anything with you people in person any further. I would appreciate if you would not trouble me in this decision.

Priya's face turned pale reading this. Even though he over exaggerated his letter, Priya was buying the stuff and was feeling guilty. Besides, I wondered why she isn't getting the

The Pragmatic

point that if Shefali isn't her real name then how on Earth Kabir found her picture on Facebook. Is she so dumb?

'I think we should try apologizing,' she said. Her eyes became moist.

'I don't think it will work. For a long time, he has been complaining that we are treating him as if he is a jerk.'

'Then?' she asked wiping her left eye with her fingers.

'Let's do what he asked for, let's leave him alone for a while,' I said as I rested my back against the pillar and sent another message to Kabir.

'You are not serious, are you?' she said raising her eyebrows.

'No, I am not. Neither now nor when I warned you that it was not a good idea to play with his emotions,' I said.

'Will you please stop this? You were equally enjoying the situation and now suddenly you are the wise boy who tried to stop me.'

'Oh, so I am the culprit now? Besides everyone knows you both hate each other.'

'When did I say that? And where the hell is this hate thing coming from?' she asked. Then followed a pause.

'It was my fault,' she said in a rather cute voice. 'It was all my fault.' Few minutes passed and still Kabir didn't come.

Priya kept crying and apologizing, repeating the same line, 'it was my fault.'

'Stop saying that and stop crying. Kabir is alright and will be here soon,' I said. 'He gave me the letter and I showed it to you, it wasn't kept here. This was just a plan to take revenge.'

'No, you are lying. I know you are lying to make me stop cry. But let me cry. I deserve it.'

'Stop it. I am not lying. We planned this stuff,' I said.

'Why would you plan this? If he wished to, he would have taken his revenge on his own. Why would you support him?' she said.

'Will you please believe me?' I asked.

'How can I? If whatever you are saying to me is true then where is Kabir? Why aren't you calling him here?'

'I tried but he is not responding.'

'Stop being childish and stop making up stories,' she said as she stood up, 'let's find him first. It's serious.' She then took out her phone.

'I will call my uncle. He is an inspector. He will help us.'

I forcefully grabbed her phone from her. 'Are you crazy? Why the hell are you calling your uncle, you moron.'

'Exactly,' she said with a smile as all her tears faded away, 'why would I call my uncle, you moron.'

'Pardon?' I said.

'Yes. That is what I said.'

'So?'

'So what?'

The Pragmatic

'Have you lost your mind?' I asked unable to comprehend what she was up to. 'Are you so dumb that you are not able to figure out that this was all just a prank?'

'Same to you,' she said and started to laugh. For a second I got scared thinking that she had lost it. But then it took me a brief moment to understand what she said.

'Are you so dumb that you are not able to figure out that this was all just a prank?' she said laughing. Kabir suddenly appeared from nowhere and joined her laughing. They gave each other a high five.

7.

It was 5.00 am and my alarm rang. At 10.00 am I had to reach the examination hall and I was anything but prepared. Previous night my eyes began to burn as I opened my textbook. The reason was, we thought it would be a good idea to watch a movie, just for half an hour, to freshen up our minds before we began. We watched the movie for about two hours and then when it ended we realised it wasn't worth watching. But already it was too late so I shut my laptop down and opened my book trying to focus. Kabir was first to surrender to sleep. He left my room asking me to wake him up early in the morning. I didn't stay up either.

Now it was 5 am and my alarm was ringing. I sat on my bed, took my phone in my hand and pressed the *snooze* button. Just five more minutes, I thought. I went back inside the blanket. One part of my brain was thinking that I should wake up. Another part suggested trusting the *snooze* button and rest. I agreed with later one.

I woke up due to continuous annoying knocking on my door.

This scared me as Kabir can never wake up so early. I looked at the window and the bright light indicated that it was late. I checked my phone, fearfully, to see how late I was.

The time displayed on the screen was 7.40 am which immediately blinked to 7.41 am, scaring me further.

The Pragmatic

Kabir entered screaming, 'you rascal, I told you to wake me up.'

I ignored him and sat on the bed. Stretched my arms took a deep breath, folded my legs, kept my elbows on my thighs and my palms on my face and started to think what went wrong

'I woke up a couple of minutes earlier,' I said.

'Then it's fine,' Kabir said and he seemed much happier. 'We both are screwed now,' he said raising his hand for a high five, I didn't raise my hand. I looked back into the book as he raised his another arm and gave himself a high five.

'How was it?' Priya asked.

'Pretty fine. It went better than my expectations,' I said and explained her the blunder we did while studying.

'I'll surely flunk,' Kabir said. 'You know what, I don't want to give any more exams.'

'Take,' Priya said, 'you don't give exams, you take exams. Anyway, these are just internal exams. You still have a good chance with the university exams.'

I didn't know that.

'I know,' Kabir said, 'next paper is on Monday, so we have a Sunday in between to study. Let's go somewhere for today.'

'Good idea,' I said looking at Priya for her approval. Three months had passed and I still struggled not to stare at her.

'Okay,' she said shrugging her shoulders, 'let's go to my place.'

'Sure,' Kabir said cheerfully, 'anyway, I am tired of eating those capsules that we will be served today in the mess.'

'I didn't invite you guys for lunch,' she said.

Kabir's face turned white.

'I am kidding,' she said laughing. 'Let's go.'

We reached the parking lot.

'Bus number 42,' she said from inside her helmet, '*Katraj-Nigdi,* you have to catch this bus. And get down at *Senadatta police station* stop.'

I hardly gave any attention to her words. Kabir was listening or at least he was pretending to. I wished I could go with her on her bike. I was thinking hard to come up with an excuse but I also knew Kabir won't let me do that.

We walked over half a kilometre to reach the *Bal-Gandharv* bus stand and waited for the 42 numbered PMT bus.

8.

'You don't like her, do you?' Kabir asked. It was the first time he had asked me this question. We were sitting at the bus stop near the Police station waiting for Priya to arrive.

'I don't like who?' I asked pretending that I didn't understand whom he was referring to.

'You know who,' he said avoiding any eye contact with me.

'No, I don't,' I said. Now I, too, was avoiding eye contact with him.

'Okay fine,' he said and turned back to his phone. I had no idea what to say. I preferred to keep quiet. We never shared such silent moments. It became little awkward. And then to my relief Priya arrived breaking the tension.

'Let's go,' she said. We followed her. She was two steps ahead and Kabir was walking with me. I wanted to go forward and talk to her. But something in me was reluctant to do so. Kabir's question was having some effect on me.

She opened the gate and we entered. The house was huge with spacious surroundings. As we walked in I noticed there were lots of plants in the surrounding, mostly flower plants which gave a splendid look to the overall structure. Her dad's BMW was parked outside.

'Beautiful,' Kabir said looking at the car. I nodded. We walked inside the door looking at the nameplate, Nishant Kulkarni, BA, L.L.B. was written on it. A young boy sat on the sofa and was watching a movie on the 40' inch LCD TV hanging on the wall.

'He is Aryan, my younger brother,' she said, 'Aryan, this is Kabir bhaiya and this is Arijit bhaiya,' we both waved a hello towards him. He smiled back.

Arijit bhaiya. She could have just said Arijit. That would have sounded much better.

We sat on the sofa as she brought two *Kokam sherbet* glasses. I looked around the hall, apart from TV there was only a picture of Priya on the front wall. The wall towards my right was filled with medals and a shelf with photographs of her father holding trophies. There were three bunches of medals and two racks full of trophies.

Adjacent to the trophies were two cupboards full of books. On the top of the first rack the word *Dad* was inscribed and on the second *Priya* using a compass. The first was filled with thick black books with golden strips.

I stood up holding the glass and went near the second rack to take a closer look at her books. Kabir was trying some tricks to get remote control from Aryan who didn't seem very much interested in Kabir. I was amazed to see her collection of books. There were many books that I have never heard of. Mostly adventure and suspense novels. No love stories, no abstract novels and not even autobiographies.

She came back replacing her jeans with white Pajama having small teddy bears all over it.

The Pragmatic

'Is that your Pajama?' I said and laughed. Meanwhile, Kabir had finally convinced Aryan and was holding the remote.

'Shut up. *Aai* brought it from her last trip to north India,' she said tying a rubber band to her hair. 'Let's go inside.'

'Can I wait here? I want to watch this movie,' Kabir asked. Aryan didn't seem very happy with it.

'No,' Priya answered, 'now lift up your asses or else I will turn off the TV.'

Kabir handed the remote to Aryan and followed Priya. I joined him.

After hall came a huge kitchen with an oversized dining table.

'How many peoples live in your house?' Kabir asked.

I waited for Priya to correct him. She never disappoints.

'People not peoples. Five: Aai, Baba, Aryan, Aaji-My Grandma and I.'

I heard voices about some argument. They stopped as we entered.

'I wasn't aware you arrived,' Mrs Kulkarni said. She was sitting with a keyboard on her lap connected to a laptop which lied aside.

'*Aai* and *Baba*,' Priya said pointing towards them.

'*Aai-Baba*, this is…,' she was interrupted by her father.

'This must be Arijit,' he said pointing towards me, 'and he must be Kabir. Good to see you, young men.'

'Hello,' I said and nodded. I was a little nervous. And a part of my brain was trying to be conscious about my every word and action. I was feeling an urge to have a good impression on them.

Kabir just smiled and nodded.

'Did we disturb you?' I asked.

'No-no, not at all,' Mr Kulkarni said. 'We were just discussing something Priya's mother is interested in writing about.'

'You are writing another article?' I asked.

'Yes,' she nodded.

'About?' I asked.

'Last week when I was travelling in a train I met a lady in my berth. She was so convinced that girls are responsible for the indecent behaviour of some boys. She was trying to convince her perception to others in the same berth.'

'And what did you say?' I asked.

'Nothing. One of the men sitting there tried to argue but she was in no mood of listening and she became aggressive when the man made some sensible points. So I decided better not to interfere,' she said. 'There are many such THINKERS in our society who will keep blaming girls for the manner in which they dress. Pathetic, isn't it?'

'Yes, it is. But unless you have some solid grounds to make your point, your article won't have any effect. It will just create a platform for more debate,' I said.

'That's what we're discussing. Something that they will relate to without doubting its righteousness,' Mr Kulkarni said.

'Try using religious examples. People rarely question our holy scriptures,' I said.

'I am not getting what you are talking about,' Priya said.

'For example, if we talked about Ramayan, can we blame Sita for being kidnapped by Ravan? Everyone will agree that it was Ravan who was the demon. Sita, too, did cross the Laxman Rekha which she wasn't supposed to do. An analogy that can be compared to the open-mindedness of our generation. And you could begin with a sarcastic title, like, *This Dussehra let's burn Sita instead.*'

'That makes sense, good,' Kabir, who was silent till this moment, said.

'Yes, well said young man,' Mr Kulkarni said.

'Thank you,' I said.

'*Baba* was very impressed by you,' Priya said as we walked out of the examination hall. Kabir was still writing his paper.

'Maybe because we both thought in the same direction,' I said.

'Not just that even *aai* was rewriting her article from scratch.'

I should have been happy hearing this but I wasn't. After visiting Priya's house, I had started feeling inferior about myself. I wasn't sure whether it was about her medals or her book shelf or the BMW that stood at her door. I also felt glad that I didn't answer Kabir's question at the bus stand truthfully.

'That's good,' I said.

'You sound strange today,' she said.

'Do I?' I asked sarcastically.

'What's the matter,' she asked.

'What are you talking about?'

'Leave it. Want to have a cup of tea?' she offered.

'Actually, I am feeling sleepy. Late night studies you know.'

'Are you leaving?' she asked.

'Yes, actually I want to have lunch before I sleep. Also, I have to study for next paper,' I said and left.

I was in my room feeling a little low about whatever I was up to. *I am trying to be practical*, I said to myself. It's better to know your limits than to get disappointed later, which could hurt even more, I thought. I started a debate within myself and was becoming restless about it.

After lunch, I tried to focus my attention in the textbook. But I was unsuccessful. So then I tried to take a nap. After a few turns on the bed, I realised it was more difficult to sleep than to study. Also, I had learnt that when we lie on the bed trying to sleep, our brains becomes more disloyal to us.

I wanted to take my mind off the subject. So I took the textbook and walked towards Kabir's room. I was about to knock when I heard some voices coming from inside. It was just Kabir's voice. I thought he is talking on his phone. I knocked. His voice suddenly stopped. He opened the door.

'With whom were you talking?' I asked.

'No one,' he said after a pause.

'I heard your voice from outside.'

'I was talking over the phone.'

'Your phone is connected to the charger in the other corner.'

Then there was a pause for about 5 seconds.

'I was singing,' he said.

'Kabir, lying is an art not everyone is capable of,' I said.

He didn't say anything. My mind was already too preoccupied to add something new.

'You sing, I didn't know that,' I said. Perhaps there were few more things that I didn't know about him.

'Sometimes,' he said, 'you are here to study?'

'No, I came here to sell this bloody textbook to you,' I said, 'want to buy?'

'Hahaha,' he faked a laugh. Something was wrong. Moreover, he was staring at the floor which signified he was trying to hide something. I ignored it.

Textbooks are not appropriate options to divert your mind. Well, a novel might help but textbooks are anything but attention seeking. And during exam period everything else seems so damn interesting.

I still found my mind thinking about Priya. The door knocked again and Kabir stood up to check who it was. I was facing the opposite direction and I didn't bother to turn back.

'Look at your book, boy,' it was Sarang Bhaiya. 'Is there anything special written on that wall, Arijit?'

'No Bhaiya, I was thinking about what I have read,' I said smiling.

'I am not your mother to believe this,' he said. 'I used to think with my eyes closed, lying on the sofa and my mother still used to believe me.'

'Not my fault Bhaiya. This subject. It's just too much for me,' I said showing him the name of the subject on the cover.

'In this case, I can help you,' he said. He was in his final year and was doing his majors in Electronics. Besides, he was amongst the scholar students in our block.

'I would love to learn from you,' I said.

'WE would love to learn from you, WE,' Kabir said.

'I have some business right now, see you after the dinner then,' he said and left.

———

I decided to have some sleep before going to Sarang's room. I slept for about two hours. My body was relaxed but my mind was still restless.

We had our dinner and were in front of Sarang's room on the first floor. Kabir knocked the door, he opened it and we went inside. His room was messy. Actually, saying this would be an understatement. His room was slovenly. At the

The Pragmatic

same time it was cool. Four speakers were playing instrumental music from the top of each corner of the room. His laptop was half opened on his bed and he was holding a copy of *'The secret of the Nagas'* in his hands. His rack was over-flooded with books. On the table was a circuit, the project on which he was working.

'How many chapters do you have for your tomorrow's paper?' Sarang asked. He was a tall and thin creature with a long face always covered with beard and white rimless spectacles on his nose.

'Five,' Kabir said. I was busy looking at his collection of books. These books were so my type, unlike Priya's collection.

'Let's start then,' he said and he looked at me, 'or shall we wait so Arijit can keep staring at the books.'

'Arijit,' Kabir said.

'Oh yeah, let's begin.'

He taught us one chapter at a time and then gave us time to revise. After that, he asked questions before moving to the next chapter. Meanwhile, he was reading his novel. He caught me every time I took my eyes off my book. Finally, he scolded me to pay some attention or else close the book and keep thinking. I tried not to look away but instead if I was thinking about something else, or about Priya, I pretended to look into the book. But mysteriously, he would catch that as well.

It was 1.30 am and we were done with questions of the fourth chapter. Kabir yawned and stood up. He rubbed his eyes, 'four chapters are enough for me,' he said as he stretched his arms making a humming sound.

'I will wait for the fifth,' I said wondering if it would be fine for me to stay there and keep him awake for one more hour. I was about to keep him awake for two more hours.

Kabir left and I closed the door as I yawned before taking my seat again. I was tired and wanted to sleep.

'If I am not wrong it's about the girl you like?' Sarang asked looking firmly into my eyes.

'I never said I liked Priya,' I said.

'And I never said I am talking about Priya,' he said.

'Yeah, but you meant the same,' I said.

'Yes, I did. And I don't think I am wrong about it. It is something about her that is bothering you, isn't' it?'

I didn't know what to say. He was too blunt and straightforward.

'Sort of,' I said looking away from him.

'You want to talk about it?'

'If you are not going to judge me.'

'Why would I judge you?' He said as he kept a bookmark in his novel, folded his legs and leaned forward towards me as if I was going to narrate him a story.

I told him everything, well, almost everything. I told him what I thought about her, that I visited her house last week, what I felt about her, about how I thought it's better to know my limits-rather-than-getting-hurt-later, etc. He listened to

The Pragmatic

everything carefully like a good student, without interrupting a single time.

I was expecting him to talk about the fact that such things happen in this age, I am not supposed to lose my focus because of such things or that it's just my hormones taking over me. Honestly, I didn't want to hear any of them. I knew all of that already. If he would have said any of these, I would have regretted having that conversation. But I didn't regret a single word in that conversation.

I kept quiet after I finished my part. Now it was his turn to speak. He gathered his thoughts and began:

'We only accept the love we think we deserve,' he said, 'I read it somewhere. And the part worth paying attention is the word *'Think'*. We don't accept the love we deserve, we accept the one which we THINK we deserve,' he said.

I remember reading this quote from the novel I was reading months ago. I was not getting what he wanted to say. But still, I nodded hoping he would elaborate further. But he didn't. He gave me some time to grasp whatever he had said. I began saying the sentence again and again in my mind until I started to understand some part of it.

'You are not ready to accept your love for her because you think you don't deserve it,' he said or probably asked, it was difficult to figure out. I nodded. But I wasn't sure whether it was appropriate for him to use the word love in the context. It sounded very heavy, very dense.

'What is it that makes you think that you are not a deserving candidate?' he asked.

Deserving candidate. I am not applying for a job to be her bodyguard. He could have used some better words, I thought.

'I don't know,' I said. I was feeling more and more uncomfortable as he started making more and more sense.

'So you have decided to maintain a polite distance from her,' he said more to himself.

'Yes,' I said. Why was he repeating my words? I knew that already.

'But you still feel restless. Still, there is some conflict inside you. In spite of the fact that you think you are doing the right thing.'

He was again repeating what I had said. I wanted to leave at this point but I collected my patience and nodded again.

'You know what that means?'

'No. But maybe because I am so used to her being with me that it will take some time for me to come back on track again.'

'Or,' he said uncrossing his legs, 'some part of you is not in agreement with whatever you are up to. Some part of your mind believes that you are the deserving candidate.'

Deserving candidate. This time, it didn't sound so bad. Actually, it sounded pretty good. Also, whatever he had said was making pretty good sense to me.

'You tried listening to your rational mind, now give a chance to your irrational mind,' he said with a cute smile making its way in the crowd of his beard. 'Give it a chance to prove that a few medals and a BMW are not something that makes you

The Pragmatic

deserve or not deserve someone. Sometimes we make some stupid choices or decisions and excuse ourselves saying that we were trying to be more rational and more practical. But this isn't being practical. This is being stupid.'

I was glad he didn't use the word *love* again, and I was also glad to have talked with him about the subject. Then for an hour or so he talked about examples of his friends, of himself and some stories from few movies and novels, trying to conclude that, eventually, it's your belief in yourself that counts. The belief, that you deserve everything you desire. I didn't pay attention to many of it, but still they were quite good.

9.

After I had the conversation with Sarang, every day was cheerful. Life seemed beautiful and all sorts of such things they say in shitty romance novels started making sense. I was able to focus on my studies again. I wrote my exams properly. No more I tried to ignore her. There wasn't a time during a day that we were not together or talking over the phone or texting each other. I kept looking for every possible reason to call her. She reciprocated the same feeling, I guess.

It was our last paper and the supervisor has thrown us out of the examination hall when she caught us talking for the third time. We waited for Priya on our regular porch. I saw her from a distance. I stared at her. Kabir looked at me while I was staring her. I noticed it but somehow it didn't matter anymore. I wanted Kabir to ask me the same question *'You don't like her?'* and I would have answered it honestly, without pretending that I didn't know who was being referred to as *her*.

Anyway, I was still staring at her image getting enlarged as she came closer. She stopped in front of me, still holding the question paper in her hand.

'I told you these questions would be asked,' she said excitedly pointing towards three questions marked in the paper, 'see.'

'And I have written all of these, thanks to you,' I said.

The Pragmatic

Kabir turned towards me angrily, 'dude, I think you should have bothered to give me the questions as well.'

'Sorry, it actually skipped my mind. Next time I will surely remember.'

'If it was *Priya* in my place I bet it wouldn't have skipped your mind,' he said stretching Priya's name.

I knew what he meant but I preferred not to say anything. This followed a silence for few seconds.

'We are going for a night out tonight,' I said breaking the silence.

'Sounds cool. Where?' she asked.

'At Kabir's friends' flat near Kothrud.'

'Great! I will be still studying for Geology paper tonight,' she said. 'Exams suck.'

'I thought you liked the subject.'

'Yes, I do like it but I don't like preparing for exams.'

'But we are free from today,' Kabir said. I was glad he finally said something.

'*Chalo*, I will leave, buh-bye. Will call you in the evening,' she said and left.

Kabir gave me a teasing look. I ignored and stood up to leave.

We had our lunch late and I was waiting for Kabir. He asked me to wait for five minutes outside the gate as he wanted to surprise me with something. He returned with someone's bike.

'Where the hell did you get this from?' I asked.

'Manoj *Mama*,' he said. Manoj was our block's night watchman. Kabir used to give his mobile loaded with movies to *Mama*- as we call him, for his entertainment in the boring night hours. Once Mama found an adult movie in Kabir's mobile and, to our surprise, he asked Kabir for more of those.

We were near the Deccan corner and Kabir was complaining about the brakes of the bike. He tried to stop near a traffic signal but was not able to do so properly, eventually, we stopped near the foot of traffic police, almost hitting his leg.

The traffic police, who seemed more to be a college student than a cop, came nearer and asked for licence and documents. I anticipated that we were about to spend some money unnecessarily. We were without a licence, without a helmet, without bike's documents, and without PUC documents. In short, we were screwed.

'You want a bribe? You son of a bitch,' Kabir said.

'Have you totally lost it?' I whispered in his ears.

The police came closer to him scanned his face carefully and broke into a hearty smile. 'You bastard,' he said, 'you came to Pune and not even bothered to call me,' and hit hard on Kabir's shoulder. 'Anyway, how is your health now? Still mental?' he asked.

The Pragmatic

Kabir didn't answer his question. I realise it was my presence that stopped him from answering. I pretended that I am not listening and looked away. They didn't talk much after that and we left.

'How come a traffic cop is your friend?'

'Actually, it's a secret.'

'A secret?'

'He is not a real cop. He is an orphan and has no source of income. Once I got him this uniform of traffic cop and since then he stands near the traffic signal taking bribes from people breaking traffic rules. I knew him since my childhood. He lived in an orphanage near our school.'

'That's so genius of you,' I said patting his back, 'and what if someone asks for a receipt?'

'He rewards them for their act against corruption by leaving them with a warning'

I laughed.

'Some people at Nashik got suspicious about him. So he transferred himself here.'

We reached our destination. Kabir started knocking.

Knock...knock...knock...knock...

A tall guy opened the door. We went inside and as soon as we entered someone switched off the light. I heard Kabir shouting some abusive words and few people hitting him very violently. I didn't know what to do so I stood there without making any noise. Then the lights were switched on. I saw Kabir who was still covered with a blanket and was in a defensive position. Everyone started to laugh and Kabir was hitting them back as they were hugging him. I felt alienated but I was still trying to fake a laugh with them.

'He is Arijit,' Kabir introduced me to his friends. 'The guy I told you about.'

'Arijit, this is...' Kabir started as one of them interrupted him.

'I am Akash,' the tall boy who opened the door said. My phone beeped. It was Priya.

'I am Raghu,' said a thin boy amongst them, who was very violent even after the lights were switched on.

'I am Vipul,' a small creature amongst them said. He offered a handshake, 'Priya is your best friend, right?' he asked after the handshake.

I wondered how he knew about Priya. Kabir gave him an angry look.

'Okay-Okay, I am not going to ask about her,' he said.

'Yes, she is a good friend,' I said and took out my phone to check the message:

Busy?

no, I replied

'Akash and Raghu are studying commerce from SP College and Vipul is studying arts from FC.'

So he is in our college. That's how he knew Priya.

The Pragmatic

Then they started talking about Nashik, their school memories, their teachers, their friends and who is studying what, the girl in the class who eloped with a local boy and all none-of-my-business stuff. I preferred to look down at my phone.

This textbook is so boring, Priya messaged.

Pity u :P. I replied. Although this time I didn't mind typing *U* instead of *You*. She was getting bored and I knew it won't matter.

They were done talking about their Nashik stuff and were now interested in knowing about me. Vipul seemed more interested in knowing about Priya, how I became friends with her, whether she was single or committed and such other shit. Kabir threw angry looks at him every time he asked any such question.

They asked me about my school, my native place and my school stories. Every time I started with a story some part of it will remind them of some incident in their school and they would end up talking about it, not giving a damn about my story. Vipul still seemed interested in listening to me or trying to become friends with me. I knew his intentions so I didn't show any interest in being friends with him.

'Kabir, you should check the new awesome stock that Vipul brought from his network,' Akash said and I immediately understood what he was referring to. Kabir seemed interested in it and went to snoop inside the laptop which Raghu was holding. Raghu pulled his laptop away, folded it and put inside his bag.

'We are not going to spend one more night just watching porn and listening to their moaning,' he said.

Kabir and Akash seemed disappointed with this. 'Let's have something to eat then,' Kabir said changing the subject.

'Tea will do?' Raghu said, 'I know a place near the railway station.'

My watch showed 2 am but I was happy with the idea of going out.

'Let's go,' I said. 'I am in.'

Everyone else nodded except Vipul. He seemed to be a lazy person.

'Let's watch some movie instead,' he said in a sluggish tone.

'I know which movie you want to watch,' Raghu said and went behind him, 'you horny bitch.' Then he gestured Kabir to get the blanket. Kabir did, till then Raghu reached near the switchboard and raised three fingers for the countdown. Everyone was looking at Raghu for his next move except Vipul who was busy explaining how Raghu was more attracted towards porn movies than him. Raghu gestured a countdown with his fingers:

Three!

Two!

One!

Lights off. Bang-bang-bang, everyone was kicking Vipul. At first, I thought I barely am friends with him so it won't be fair to hurt him. But then he had asked about Priya and thus it became my duty or right, or whatever it might be, to hurt him. I did. I kicked him hard in his butt. He screamed loudly. After lights were turned on I was still kicking him. In fact, I was the only one still kicking him. He looked at me from below, held my right leg, pulled me down on the floor. Lights were turned off again and this time, the blanket was over me.

10.

'Glad to see you not talking with that saddening girl on your phone again,' Kabir said, 'I am warning you she is not a good girl, you will later regret.'

'Don't start again,' I said and I was irritated by the conversation he was about to start again. 'Can't we talk about anything else?'

'Okay we will talk about something you like, first let's go out and sit on that bench,' he pointed towards the bench near my room.

So now we were sitting on the bench silently looking around our hostel block. Fergusson College hostels were one of the oldest structures in the city. The construction was done in a classic style. The structure was rectangular, with the rooms covering the perimeter and the central region was left open, with a tree and a bench at each corner and a large metallic pole with light bulbs in the centre, lighting the area.

He was silent but was up to something. This was quite clear from his body language.

'You were about to say something that we will like,' I said.

'No, I said we will talk something you will like,' he said.

'Same stuff.'

'It's not same. See if you say…'

'Focus man, focus. Come to the point.'

'Now, if you have decided that you are not going to listen to me…'

'I don't want to listen to the same stuff again, for god's sake, can't you understand I am not interested to know why you don't like her,' I said.

'Listen. Listen…' he said interrupting me, 'what I am saying is that, I think it's the right time to talk to her.'

'About?'

'You know what.'

'No, I don't.' I lied.

He gave me a horrible look.

'Okay, I know what you are talking about,' I said, 'but what makes you think so?'

'You are a dumb boy in this matter and I know you will never take an initiative on your own, neither Priya is going to talk anything regarding this.'

'Don't you think it's too early?'

'I am not asking you to propose her for marriage, just make it clear from your side that what your intentions are.'

'Intentions? What do you mean by that?' I asked, 'I have nothing sort of "Intentions" regarding her. I am happy being her friend for the time being concerned.'

'Chill man, don't get me wrong.'

'You better keep your freaking mouth shut. Got it?'

'Sure. But just imagine for a moment that Priya, being a girl, is waiting for you to approach her. And you, with all your good intentions, are waiting for the right M-O-M-E-N-T. God knows what that means. She may think that you are not interested in her. She may think that you just want to remain friends with her. Basically, imagine you are screwing up your very moment with her, thinking that this is not the right time.'

'You know, you are not making sense,' I said but I felt that at least some part of whatever he said was making a hell lot of sense.

'Look,' he said with a very intense voice, 'look at me and say that I don't know what I am talking about and that whatever I said is insane. I promise I will never bring this topic up again.'

I sighed.

'Well, you make some sense.'

'Some? I make hundred percent sense.'

'Not hundred percent, fifty-fifty.'

'Fifty? No way.'

'Well, let's settle for sixty-five.'

'Seventy-five and it's a deal?'

'Okay done. So seventy-five percent of whatever you said made sense.'

'Thank you for kind deal, now let's get back to the point.'

'Sure,' I nodded.

'31st will be a perfect date.'

'No way, you are not saying that I should do it on my...'

'Yes. I am saying this,' Kabir said interrupting me.

30th October. 11:59 pm.

I looked at the time on the mobile screen as I heard the crinkling sound made by plastic bags outside my room along with the *ssshhh* sound made to stop that crinkling.

The date on the screen blinked to 31st and they all started banging my door loudly with their fists and legs. I opened the door and everyone entered shouting Happy Birthday and hugging me turn by turn. I saw Kabir placing three large plastic bags in the corner. I pretended that I didn't notice. Suraj came close to hug me and then he did what I hated the most. He kissed me on my left cheek. He was apparently not satisfied with that because then he held my face twisted it and kissed me on my right cheek. I wanted to kick him for this but it was my birthday and I was supposed to tolerate everything.

It was getting noisy. Mayank, the most sincere guy from our block who used to wear glasses that were so thick that I wondered whether a bullet can pass through them, asked everyone to maintain silence as *Mama*, our watchman, may complain about the midnight chaos to our Rector.

Everyone ignored him.

Kabir came and hugged me. It was a warm hug and I felt it deeply.

'Happy Birthday,' he whispered in my ear. I was expecting that he too will be making my cheeks dirty by pasting his saliva on them. But he didn't, maybe he didn't want to touch his lips to already wet cheeks. Whatever may be the reason I felt happy that he didn't kiss me.

Mayank again asked everyone to lower their voices.

Everyone ignored him.

Kabir lifted the first plastic bag and asked Akshay to make some space on the study table. Akshay nodded and within seconds moved his fist over the study table without even looking what was there and cleaned the table. Kabir lifted the cake packed in a brown cheap looking box and kept it on the table.

I sat on the bed and the table was kept in front of me with a cake on it. I wondered why my name was not written on the cake. I wondered why I was focusing on the name and the cheap looking stuff. I wondered why nobody offered me a knife. I wondered why Mayank was again asking everyone to be quiet. And again,

Everyone ignored him.

My phone started ringing. I tried to reach it when someone pulled it away and placed it inside my bag switching it on silent mode.

'Good,' Kabir said to him, 'Arijit, now make a wish.'

I closed my eyes but before I can think of anything I felt my nose rubbing in the mud of cream with some hands

The Pragmatic

forcefully pushing back of my head. It was getting harder to breathe so I banged my fist on the table. Thankfully, the grip of the hand on my head loosened and I raised my face to breathe. I removed my spectacles and Kabir placed my cake covered spectacles on the rack. I wiped my eyes and within seconds my face was again in the cream this time with a harder bang. I could sense everyone was enjoying this show with their voices cheering and getting louder. I thought my nose would start bleeding anytime.

'Keep your voices down, you Assholes,' Mayank shouted loud enough to wake up Mama from his midnight nap.

No one ignored him. All were silent.

After getting my nose banged for three times those few seconds of silence were wonderful. I cleared my face and to my surprise found that someone was knocking the door. I sighed thinking that this could be Mama. Mayank opened the door and a friendly voice asked, 'am I late?'

It was Sarang.

'You are perfectly on time,' Kabir said as he lifted the table and placed it in a corner.

I looked with suspicious eyes. No way, no more violence, I thought.

'Time for some birthday bumps,' Suraj announced and turned off the lights.

In no time I was dragged on the floor and people were making their way through the crowd to grab a chance to kick me in every possible place. Then I felt the grip holding my hands becoming looser so I pulled myself away but still the voices were not down and someone was screaming.

'It's me you Rascals,' Mayank said. I knew they intentionally dragged him in, nevertheless, he rescued me again.

The table was arranged again and the second plastic bag was opened. It contained a blue coloured Monginis box, inside the box was a chocolate flavoured cake. I made a wish, this time with my eyes wide open and cut the cake, they were singing the Happy Birthday song. I fed the first piece to Kabir, then to Sarang, and then to others.

Kabir's phone started ringing and I immediately realised who must be calling him.

'Silence everyone, *Bhabhiji* is calling,' he shouted. I caught his phone and received the call. As soon as I did this, everyone in the room started to sing in chorus.

'I am calling you since fifteen minutes, where the hell did you bury your phone?' Priya screamed over the phone. 'And what is this noise?'

'Nothing. I am having a birthday celebration and they took my phone away to avoid disturbances. And this noise is because they are teasing me.'

'Teasing you for what?'

'You ask a lot of questions.'

'Shut up. Anyway how is your celebration going? Did Kabir gave you the gift?'

'Not yet,' I said.

'Whoops!' she said.

The Pragmatic

'And?'

'And you are giving us a treat tomorrow.'

'Sure, after lectures. You decide the place.'

'Okay, done.'

'And?'

'And nothing else, going to sleep. Sweet dreams.'

'Okay bye, good night.'

'Good night,' she said and hung the phone.

I entered the room and everyone was nodding and making a humming sound. I tried not to blush.

Then Kabir's phone rang again. It was Priya. I left the room again ignoring whatever sound they were making this time.

'Hello,' I said in a surprised voice.

'Happy Birthday, I forgot to wish you. So stupid of me.'

'Yeah. It is indeed stupid,' I said.

'Shut up. The noises in the background singing that song distracted me.'

'Okay, okay don't start again, thank you very much.'

'What do you mean by don't start again?'

'Nothing. We will continue tomorrow, for now, go to sleep, madam.'

'Sure. Babye, and once again happy birthday.'

'Thank you. Bye.'

After finishing the cake and vote of thanks, everyone except Kabir and Sarang left.

Kabir opened the third plastic bag. Only three of us were in the room. He handed me a box wrapped in shiny coloured paper. I was frightened to see that he actually gift-wrapped something.

I tore the wrapping and found a photo frame, with a recent photograph of Kabir and me with his hands over my shoulder. I laughed when I remembered the original photograph.

'You cropped the photograph,' I said, 'you cropped her out.'

'Yes, I did,' he said.

'But it's good, it's damn good. Thank you,' I said and it was one of the rare times when we say thank you and we really mean it. And during such times 'Thank you' sounds so meaningless, but still it was the best I could say.

Then it was Sarang's turn. He pulled out a diary from the same plastic bag, it wasn't wrapped with fancy paper and handed it to me. It was a beautiful notebook sized diary with spiral binding. The cover was hand sketched. The sketch was of a teen boy holding a pen in his hand, looking away and lost in his thoughts. I opened it and was surprised by what was written on it:

To,
The Secret Poet

'How do you know this?' I asked him.

The Pragmatic

'Made a pretty guess!' he said smiling, 'or maybe I read one of your poems which you wrote on the back of the book you gave me to read.'

'Silly me,' I said.

'Dude you never told me you write poems,' Kabir said. He, too, sounded surprised.

'Believe me, it's not a big deal I just wrote a few pathetic poems,' I said and looked at Sarang Bhaiya, 'which doesn't make me a Secret Poet.'

'Whatever. From now you can write your pathetic poems in this diary. It's way better than writing on the back of some random books.'

'Thank you,' I said and turned the cover page and found that there were few lines written on the second page, 'and now what's this?'

'It's a cut-out from my first poem and coincidentally it is the answer to the questions you raised in your poem,' he said.

I almost ignored whatever he said and began reading, the lines were-

Not warmth she was,
but just the fur.
He was into her,
but he loved the way he loved her.

'Well, I must say, I guessed that you might be writing poetry,' I said trying to avoid making any comments on the lines.

'Can I see?' Kabir asked and pulled the diary.

'You wrote this after your break-up?' Kabir asked after reading the lines.

'First. After my first break up when I realised that she wasn't the end of the world and when I started falling for another one.'

'It's good, pretty good actually. I will like to read the complete poem,' Kabir said.

'Actually, it's not complete yet,' he replied.

'What? When did you have your first break up?' I asked.

'When I was in eighth grade.'

'Wait a minute. That must be around seven years ago!' I said.

'Dude you are writing a poem since last seven years, and you think we'll believe this shit?' Kabir asked.

'I write one paragraph after my every breakup. And I am not sure which will be my last break up.' He was smiling.

'How many paragraphs have you written so far?' Kabir asked.

'Six.'

'That's cool,' Kabir said.

'And you? How many paragraphs are there in your poem,' he asked Kabir.

'One. One stupid and sour paragraph,' Kabir said, 'by the way, today Arijit is going to start writing his first paragraph.'

'Sounds good.'

The Pragmatic

I was quiet and had no interest in talking about Priya. I was already thinking about her for a very long time and my mind was saturated with her thoughts.

'Thank you for the gift,' I said trying to divert the conversation.

Sarang got up from his seat to leave. 'Seems like someone doesn't want to talk about something. Anyway, good luck for tomorrow,' he said and left.

Kabir gave me some advice which I found irrelevant. After talking for more half an hour he was ready to leave.

'Tell me about what you mentioned as your first paragraph, tell me about the girl,' I said.

'Look,' he said in a very intense and serious tone. I had never seen him so serious.

'Few things you are not supposed to ask,' he said narrowing his eye, 'this is one such bloody shit you will never ask about.'

I was feeling quite scared about the way he said that. 'Okay, calm down,' I said waving my hands to calm his temper.

'I am sorry,' he said and left. I was shocked by his response.

'Never mind,' I thought as I washed my face and then I tried to have some sleep as there was a big day lying ahead of me. But I hardly slept. I was imagining the scenario. What I would say, how she would react, how I would respond to her reactions, which words would have a more profound effect, what to say and what not to say.

11.

I woke up and looked around, again it was totally dark. I picked the clothes lying on the floor and wore them. I had no idea how long I had slept or for how long I had been here. I had no idea what was going to happen with me. Are they going to kill me after they are done with me? Or worse, are they going to continue this forever?

Outside world had become a fantasy for me. The last thing I remember was getting mad at Arijit as he was not receiving my call. I was scared again as I walked through the same street. I felt that someone was following me. I started to walk at a faster pace. As I did he yelled some name and the guy standing in front of me grabbed my hand.

'No. she is not our girl,' he said as I was trying to push him away. I began to run as soon as he released my hand.

'I don't care. Just get her and I will give you whatever you will ask for.'

The guy who held my hand suddenly appeared from nowhere. He slapped me hard and I fell on the road. He lifted me and carried me towards a nearby room where someone covered my mouth and nose till I became unconscious. I don't remember anything further. When I regained my consciousness I was in the room.

The door crinkled again. The short guy came in and lit the room.

'You need anything to eat? We are going out,' he asked. I ignored him and looked away.

The Pragmatic

'I am talking to you, bitch,' he shouted. I didn't look at him.

'As you wish,' he said and left. I heard voices from the other room. The door opened and closed, then the sound of footsteps faded away. I thought of trying to escape but then they might have taken care of it so I didn't bother to check the other room. I sat on the bed thinking about how my life is going to be. At that point of time, I had lost hopes that anyone will ever find me or that I will be able to meet again the people I loved so much. Even after a few years, when I will be independent enough to leave this place, will I be able to face them? Will they accept me?

Suddenly, I thought if there would be a telephone in the room next to mine, I would be able to call Baba. I stood up and slowly reached the door, opened it a little bit and snooped into the other room checking if anyone was there. Both of them had left. I opened the door completely and walked into the room. On my right were three iron beds having a filthy curtain wall between each of them. On my left was a small television, a DVD player and a rack of CDs. Opposite to this was a small broken couch with many alcohol bottles lying next to it. The room was stinking of alcohol and rotten eggs. I went near the door and tried to open it but it was locked. I kicked it but then realised I should not make any noise. I looked around for any telephone or mobile devices but there were none. Then I checked the drawers in the DVD table.

I pulled the first drawer, there was nothing inside it. The second contained packets of cigarette, match boxes and lighters. The third drawer contained a large number of condoms of different flavours and manufacturers. Three gone, three more to check, I thought. The fourth drawer had a treasure for me inside it. I got my cell phone in it, dissembled. I collected all the parts but the sim card was missing. I cursed my luck. I checked other two drawers but they were empty. I bent down to look for my sim under the table. I saw something which looked like a sim card. It was just a few centimetres away from my reach.

There was some noise at the door and I quickly gathered all parts of my phone and ran towards my room. I hid them under the pillow and pretended to be asleep. There were some noises coming from the other room of men talking. Two voices were known but the third was new. This scared me and I immediately started to shiver. I knew what was going to happen. My eyes were already wet and I started to pray.

The door crinkled and the thin boy came in. He was accompanied by the stranger. I know what was going to happen. As the stranger came in, the boy closed the door and left. I collected myself and sat on the corner pleading, weeping and begging him to stop there.

'Don't worry,' he said as he came closer to the bed.

'Please, please,' I screamed ignoring what he said, 'please go away, I beg.'

'Don't worry,' he said again, 'I am not here to do anything you are thinking about.'

I didn't say anything. He moved closer and sat on the bed. I started to shiver again.

'I am here because my friends sent me here,' he said and folded his legs on the bed. 'They forced me in. This man is their regular guy. I would just sit here for a while and then I will leave.'

I was very much relieved hearing this. I still said nothing but I was less scared now and my shivering had also stopped. He seemed to be a nice guy. I thought he could help me to contact my parents.

The Pragmatic

First few minutes were silent and he was checking the place. When he was done, he broke the silence.

'How much are you paid? I mean if you are not allowed to answer its fine,' he asked.

I started to cry harshly.

'They kidnapped me,' I said holding my tears.

'What the hell! Poor you. Can I help you to get away from here?'

'Will you do that? I mean yes. Just give me your phone,' I said. *Suddenly all my hopes were alive again.*

'He took my phone before I entered. Now I know why he did that. Give me someone's phone number to whom I can inform about you.'

'Sure,' I said. *I searched the room but there was no pen or paper. I took my mobile from beneath the pillow and assembled the battery and the body.*

'Take this, it has all the contact numbers. Call my dad first. Contact name is Baba,' I said and handed the phone to him, 'it doesn't have a sim card in it.'

But then I thought that this phone is everything I have, and if this boy didn't call my dad, I will get stuck here for the rest of my life. The risk was too big.

'Or,' I said, 'can you share your internet with me when you take your phone from him?'

'Sure I can. But you think it will work?'

'Yes it will, I can message a lot of people simultaneously,' I said as he handed me back my phone.

He asked a few more questions about me and kept talking about himself for twenty more minutes. I hardly paid attention. My mind was busy thinking about getting away from here. He stood up to leave.

'Thank you,' I said, 'and remember to switch on your hot-spot.'

'Yes and you're welcome,' he said and closed the door.

I switched on my mobile, it asked for time and date. I was feeling so helpless about not knowing the exact date and time. Nevertheless, I skipped the part and turned on my Wi-Fi and waited for him to do his part. I saw his hot-spot network and tried to connect.

And shit. It asked for a password. How can I forget to ask him the password? I ran towards the door and as I opened it I saw the two guys lying on the couch and watching a cricket match on TV. As soon as I opened the door they both looked at me in surprise.

'Water, can I get some water?' I asked. The boy I was looking for was not in the room. He must be standing outside.

The short guy stood up and brought me a bottle of water. I took a sip and faked a cough.

'May I go outside for a walk?' I asked thinking that if I managed to get outside, I will be able to ask him the password.

'May I fuck you?' he asked and both of them started to laugh.

'I just want some fresh air, I am suffocating here.'

'Do we look stupid? Get back inside or I will take you in and will stay with you there for some time,' he said and looked away at the TV.

The Pragmatic

I wanted to run but I knew it was the most stupid thing to do. Then resisting the temptation to run, I returned to the room. I looked at my phone's screen. The Wi-Fi network was available for five more minutes, then it disappeared. So did my hopes. But I still had my phone in my hand and I knew that my sim card was below the table.

12.

'Cynophobia,' Priya said.

'And what's that?' I asked. Kabir and I were narrating her the incident when dogs were chasing us on a lonely road at about 2 a.m. in the morning.

'It's a morbid fear of dogs,' she explained, 'I would have fainted there watching so many dogs chasing me.'

Kabir's phone started to ring. I didn't know who was calling him but I was grateful to that person for helping us in Kabir's plan. As per our plan, he left saying that one of his friend had come and was in need of some money, urgently.

'I will join you guys in twenty minutes,' he lied and left.

We were sitting in the Good luck cafe to celebrate my birthday.

'I think we should wait for him,' Priya said.

I didn't think about this.

'His twenty minutes may turn out being two hours. Besides, you are starving. I think there is no point in waiting.'

'You are right. Let's order something,' she said, 'what will you like to have mister birthday boy?'

Well, I had imagined this situation where both of us were sitting alone, but in my imagination, things were lot different. I didn't imagine I would feel so nervous raising the topic, I didn't imagine people sitting so close that they might listen to our conversation, and I didn't imagine she would look so beautiful that day and I didn't imagine I would start over thinking and worrying.

'I asked what you would like to have.'

'Anything will be fine for me,' I said avoiding an eye contact.

'Okay,' she said and placed the order for both of us. I didn't even hear what she said.

She wore a black one piece dress. It was the first time I saw her exposing so much of her body. She looked seductive. But all that made me more nervous. Couldn't she just wear normal clothes? After all it was my birthday, not her.

Meanwhile, my mind was offering all the possible excuses to run away from this situation. I had met her just a few months ago and was being impatient, I should spend some more time with her before asking her. She once told me about her best friend who asked her out. They were in school then. She refused his proposal and hadn't talked to him since. All such thoughts were offered by my brain to run away.

'Arijit,' she almost shouted, 'why are you so lost today?'

'I am sorry, did you say something?'

'What's wrong with you?'

'Nothing.'

'Sure?'

'Hmm,' I muttered, 'you were saying something.'

'No, I wasn't.'

'Fine, then say something.'

'What's wrong Arijit?'

I sighed. 'I want to talk about something.'

'And what's preventing you from doing so?'

'Nothing.'

'So go on. Speak up.'

'Look,' I said.

'There is something I want you to know,' I said. Her face turned blank and clueless.

'What?'

I sighed.

'That I like you'.

I sighed again.

I finally said it and I felt very lighter. I didn't know I did a right thing or a wrong one, but at that time it felt so good.

'And I won't be asking you to answer this because it's less sort of question and more sort of an affirmation,' I said. I had recited my lines very well and so far haven't made any blunder. Her expressions were like I was talking in a foreign language and she had no idea what I was talking about.

An awkward silence followed. She kept looking at her plate avoiding any eye contact.

The Pragmatic

After waiting for like forever, I broke the silence.

'You can say something,' I said.

'Can we talk about it later?' she asked.

'Sure.'

Rest of the time we ate in silence and talked very little.

―――

We walked towards college's parking lot where she had parked her bike. Kabir didn't join us. My thoughts were running between whether I screwed things up or I did the right thing. I was not going to figure this out for the rest of my life.

We reached near her bike.

'You planned this whole thing, didn't you?' she asked, 'I mean, Kabir leaving us alone, your birthday treat and all.'

'Yes,' I said feeling guilty.

'Let's finish our talk,' she said. It was good to see smile returning on her face.

'We can talk later if you want,' I said. Now I wanted to procrastinate this talk.

'No, it's fine.'

'I mean it. If you want we can talk tomorrow or so,' I said.

'Shut up and listen,' she said in a harsh voice, 'I know you are a bit sentimental person and that your feelings are dominant in your every decision, but I want you to think practically about whatever I am going to say.'

So I was a sentimental boy and my feelings were dominating me.

'I knew you like me, and I never thought you will admit it and that too so impatiently, can't you have some patience?'

I was thinking about Kabir and was wishing to kick him hard. Meanwhile, I just nodded and waited for her to arrive at the point.

'Well, and now that you have said that, let me make it clear that even though I feel the same about you I don't think this is a proper time to get engaged in such stuff.'

'And what does that mean?' I asked.

'That means, that yes I like you but for the time being, I will prefer we remain best friends and we'll think about it later.'

'Okay, that sounds pretty sane,' I said but I didn't mean it. It didn't sound sane neither it was insane. It was just confusing me.

She unhooked her helmet from her bike and just before she sat on the bike she did the most beautiful thing of the evening.

She came close to me and hugged me tightly. It was a very short hug but was tight and sweet. Neither did she say anything nor did I. She left and I was staring at her fading image when suddenly she stopped. She looked towards me and waved me calling me where she stopped. I went there. She removed her helmet.

'Don't you want a present?' She asked.

'Of course, I do.'

'I almost forgot,' she opened her bag and removed a gift wrapped box from it.

'Am I supposed to open it now?'

'Yes.'

I unwrapped it and found a box. I opened the box and was delighted to see what was inside it.

It was a wooden Rubik's cube with six photographs instead of colours on the sides. It was scrambled so it was difficult to identify the pictures but I could see faces on some random blocks. I could see my face, Priya's face and even Kabir's face. I wanted to show this to Kabir as she had included his photo.

'Thank you,' I said, 'I mean it.'

'You are most welcome,' she said politely, 'buh-bye'.

She left.

13.

'Arijit,' Priya was on the line.

'Yes, ma'am.'

'Can we talk for a while?'

'Sure. What happened?'

'I am little scared right now, thought will feel better talking to you.'

'Scared? What happened? Where are you?'

'Don't overreact, okay? I think I am in the *peth* area.'

Pune city was filled by *'peth'* areas. Apparently, people here took every word they liked and added a suffix *peth* to name localities of the city. They even named places suffixing names of weekdays with the *Peth* word. I would have got confused about which exact *peth* she was referring to, but her asking me not to overreact gave me some hint.

'W-h-i-c-h *peth*?' I asked slowly emphasizing the words.

'Budhwar peth,' she said hesitatingly.

'In the red light area?' I frowned.

'Yes, think so. I have never been here earlier so not quite sure about it.'

'What the hell are you doing there? You know it's not a good place for girls.'

'Are you saying it's a good place for boys?'

'Let me rephrase my sentence, it's not a safe place for girls. Don't try to distract me. What the heck are you doing there?'

'I am going to my Grandma's place.'

'Your Grandma lives there? Who is she?' I asked without thinking.

'Mind your words Arijit,' she sounded angry.

'I am sorry. I just got carried away.'

'It's okay. *Aaji* lives nearby. My bike ditched me again so I took a detour from my regular way and found a shortcut. But there were stray dogs fighting in the lane from where I was supposed to go, so I looked around for an alternate path and ended up here.'

'You choose this path instead of crossing stray dogs?'

'Cynophobia. You know, I've told you about.'

'Yes, I do.'

'Anyway, I am almost out of these place.'

'You are not going to use the same path on your way back, are you?'

'Of course not, provided there aren't any dogs on my way back.'

'Dogs will do nothing, you should be more precautious about men. They are more dangerous.'

'Okay-Okay I will allow dogs to insert their sharp teeth inside my soft flesh, but won't dare to come here. Is that a deal?'

'Yes, it is,' I said, 'and you better mind it.'

'Okay,' she said. It was an *okay* we say when we disagree with our parents, we know we are not going to do whatever they are asking us but still to pass the moment we say *okay* in agreement.

'And if you did, you know I will scold you but still if you feel scared you are going to call me. Is that a deal?'

'Yes sir,' she said, 'bye now, I am standing near Aaji's building for a while.'

'Bye,' I said.

'Wait- wait-wait,' she screamed.

'What?'

'Well, I wasn't going to tell you about this but listen anyway. I have a present for you'

'Wow! That sounds cool. What is it?'

'You're not supposed to ask what your gift is.'

'Oh yeah, sure. Don't tell me,' if she didn't want me to know, why the hell was she talking about it?

'But listen anyway. It's a letter,'

'Are you serious? You wrote a love letter?'

'It's not a love letter.'

'Then?'

'It's a note I wrote after reading a novel, I thought you will like it.'

'You have started reading love stories, haven't you?' I asked smiling.

'Bye now I'm getting late,' she said and ended the call.

I looked at the digital clock on my screen. It was 8.30 pm and I guessed she would be back at the same place, if she did, at around ten pm which was not a good time to be there.

'You did what?' I asked in a surprised tone.

'Not my fault. He was the one who parked his car in the no-parking zone,' Kabir said. We were sitting on his bed. Prof Bharadwaj had parked his car in a No-parking zone and the officers chained the car and wrote a contact no with a chalk on the window. Kabir *grabbed this opportunity*, as he termed it, and erased the number on the window.

'Mind blowing job,' I patted his back, 'how was his reaction?'

'For first few minutes he was in shock thinking who chained his car. Then his fellow friend suggested that some official might have done this as he parked in the wrong place. His temper rose and he started abusing the officers who didn't bother to write the contact number.'

'And then?'

'Then I shot his video in which the so-called Prof Bharadwaj, who is well known for his sophisticated attitude, is caught cursing. I have forwarded this video to every WhatsApp group I am in,' he sounded so proud of what he had done, 'I wish you and Priya were along to see his face.'

That reminded me Priya hadn't called me as she was supposed to do. I put my hand in my pocket to reach my phone but then I realised that I forgot to bring my phone along. I rushed into my room and checked my phone. It had seven missed calls. Four were of Priya's dad's, two of her mom's and the last was of Priya's. I called her first but her phone was switched off. Then I called on her Dad's number.

'Hello Arijit, Priya's dad here.'

'Yes, uncle.'

'Did you talk with Priya today in the evening?'

I hesitated, 'y-e-s.'

'What time?'

'Around half past eight, uncle. When she was on her way to her grandma's place.'

'Oh,' he sounded disappointed.

'What happened uncle?'

'She left her grandma's place more than an hour ago and hasn't reached home yet. Also, her phone is switched off.'

'Her bike ditch… I mean her bike was giving some trouble. She might have taken it to some garage for repairing.'

'She told me about the bike. I found it at the place where she mentioned. I am at her grandma's house but I didn't see her on the way. You have any idea where she might have gone?'

I thought for a while whether to mention about her passing through the red light area.

'Uncle, she went through the red light zone. Take a look there as well.'

'What?' he screamed. I could imagine him jumping on his seat.

'Actually…'

I narrated the story.

'I will ask her every friend I know. Just give me a call when you find her and don't worry uncle she will be perfectly fine.'

I locked my room. It was 10.30 pm and the hostel gates were closed. There was no way out. I went back to Kabir's room, 'do anything but get us out quickly.'

'You have to be there in ten, you understand? It's serious,' Kabir was talking to his friends on his phone.

'Let's go,' he said.

'What's the plan?' I asked, 'how are we going to get out?'

'Begging,' he said and turned towards the hostel gate where Mama was sitting and rubbing some tobacco in his palm with his fingers.

We explained everything to him. He seemed to be believing us.

'Are you asking permission to go that place at this time of night?'

We were silent.

'What if something happens to you? Take my advice and stay away from girl's matters. Or go in the morning, I can't let you go on my risk.'

'We want to go on our risk,' I said.

'Boy, if something happens to you or even if nothing happens to you and Rector Sir comes to know that I let you go, imagine what he will do with me.'

Again there was silence.

'What if you are not aware? I mean that if we are not here when the gates were closed. You can say this if we got caught. I promise we won't drag you in.'

This made him angry, 'don't try to be over smart. A no simply means a no. Now you better lift up your asses and get inside your rooms.'

'We understand that they are strict with you mama and you will lose your job if you allowed us to go,' I began, 'and I pity you for this. I also pity you about tomorrow, because when they will know about you getting intoxicated during your working hours and keeping your alcohol bottles in senior student's room, you will definitely lose your job.'

'You cannot blackmail me,' he said.

'We don't even want to,' Kabir said.

'What do you want?'

'To get out of here.'

He looked around and without making any noise opened the gate. We rushed out.

'Don't come back tonight,' he shouted on our back. We ignored and ran towards the gate.

Three bikes were waiting outside the college gate. Vipul, Raghu, Akash and Michael, the traffic police guy, had shown up on time. I sat on Raghu's bike, Kabir sat on Akash's and Vipul was on Michael's bike.

'What's the matter?' Raghu asked as we headed towards the JM road.

'It's about Priya...' I said and was interrupted by Michael.

'Don't tell me we are going to have a fight with some jerks who are troubling her?' he asked.

'No, for god's sake listen to him,' Kabir said.

'Priya was passing by the *Budhwar Peth* at around nine thirty pm and she is missing since then,' I said.

'What the hell she was doing there?' Akash asked.

'Who is Priya?' Michael asked.

'Priya is our friend and what she was doing there is a long story.' Kabir offered.

'To be brief, in an attempt to find an alternate path for where she was going, she ended up in a wrong place,' I said.

We were near the corporation building and it was raining heavily. No one amongst us was wearing a raincoat or jacket. I was shivering with cold or because of fear.

'You have her photo on your phone?' Vipul asked.

'Yes, I have,'

'Then WhatsApp it to Kabir,' he replied, 'Kabir, forward it to rest of us, we will all need a photo of her.'

I did.

Was it real? Was it actually happening? I wished not, but it was. The thought that where she might be now and in what situation was scaring me further. All sort of negative thoughts were striking my mind. I just hoped that things will not turn out the way I was thinking. I hoped that after an hour or so we will be sitting somewhere and scolding her about the mischief she did.

I called her father to get the update.

'Uncle, Arijit here.'

'Yes,' he sounded so depressed that it was not necessary to ask him anything further.

'Did you check whether she arrived home?'

'We sent our neighbours. They are keeping a watch over there.'

'We will be reaching there in fifteen minutes. Have you contacted police station?'

'I am in contact with an Inspector who is a relative of a client of mine. He will be reaching here anytime,' he sounded horrified.

The Pragmatic

'We will keep on looking till he arrives, call me if you get to know something,' I said trying not to sound as afraid as I was.

'Sure,' he said and hung the phone.

It started to rain heavier. I pushed the phone in my pocket and wiped my tears. As every minute passed things were getting worse. I wanted all these things to end-up, like a nightmare ends. I wanted to slap her for her misbehaviour. I wanted to scold her for not listening to me. I wanted to get mad at her. And above all, I wanted to see her right away.

I saw Vipul trying to say something.

'Don't worry, she will be fine. We will find her, I promise you,' he said.

But words, however pleasant they might sound, were not going to make things any better.

I nodded.

We parked our bikes and were standing opposite to Kaka Halwai sweet shop.

'Everyone is having a photo of her with them?' Michael asked.

We all nodded.

'Listen now, I will take Arijit with me and we will talk to *Akka*. Let's see whether that brat helps us. Mostly she won't. Meanwhile, try to find out the dealers here and tell them we will offer any amount they will ask for. If she is here we better find her quickly,' he added.

Who was *Akka*? Who were the dealers? How were we supposed to deal with those people? And how come Michael knew so much about this place?

All these questions were running through my mind. But I thought it would be better to keep quiet and follow the guy, who seemed to know what he was talking about.

'Arijit, one last time, you're sure she was here at that time?' Akash asked me just when we were about to leave.

'Probably,' I cleared my throat, 'I am not certain about anything.'

'But the risk is too big to ignore that she might be behind any of these walls,' Kabir added.

'Look, they don't kidnap girls from here. They don't want to welcome police, if not as their customers. Generally, the girls are brought from some other cities or villages,' Michael said.

I was quiet. So was everyone else.

'It will be a great news if she is not here. Let's hope they will find her near her house or somewhere. But given the circumstances, we should search this place first,' Kabir said.

'You're right, let's begin,' I said.

Kabir and Vipul chose the first lane, Raghu and Akash took the next. Michael asked me to follow him. As I followed I saw a woman to my right. She was oversized and was very unusual. Her lipstick shade was too bright and she had put up thrice the amount she should have. The kohl in her eyes was overextended towards the edges and was too dark. She

The Pragmatic

was not wearing a single ornament, not even a thread in her neck. Vermillion was absent from the line of partition of her hair and she was dressed in a very indecent way.

She was looking towards me. I realized that I was staring at her for a long time so I suddenly took my eyes off her. As we walked further, I discovered that there were many such hideous women around. Maybe hundreds of them, maybe thousands. Equal in number were men, bursting with testosterones and hunger of lust. Mostly they were drunk or apparently frustrated.

Michael asked me to walk quietly keeping my eyes open and mouth shut. He will be doing all the talking stuff. We reached a small tenement. The door was open and a young boy was standing outside.

'*Akka?*' Michael asked him.

'Who are you?' he opened his stinky mouth which smelled of cheap liquor.

'None of your business.'

'Get lost.'

Michael held his phone in his hand and showed him the photo of Priya, 'we are looking for her.'

'You won't find such cheeks here,' he said with a wicked smile.

'Can I have a word with *Akka?*' Michael asked again.

'You may try your luck,' he said and moved away from our way.

'We don't kidnap women. They are here by their own will,' she said after Michael explained her the purpose of our visit. She was a dark and oversized woman, must be in her early fifties. She was different from other women around in a sense that she was without lipstick and kohl overflowing through her lips and eyes.

But that didn't make her look any decent. Her eyes were horrible and scary. She wore a pair of golden coloured bangles, though it was not real gold, and a thick golden chain around her neck. Her accent was worse than anyone I had heard so far and she was anything but polite with us.

Michael talked in a serious tone, 'we have money. We will give whatever amount you will ask for. Just find her, she must be here. You are the only one who can do this. We won't file a complaint and the matter will be closed right here. Just get her for god's sake.'

'Leave your number. I will ring you if I get to know anything,' she said, 'by the way, who is she? Your sister or something?'

'She is his friend,' Michael said pointing towards me.

'Oh, I see,' she nodded narrowing her eyes, 'must be a special friend. Take my advice, stay as far as possible from your friend.'

'Sure,' Michael said and stood up before I could respond to whatever she said.

'If Priya is kidnapped here by any of the dealers, she must be knowing,' Michael said sounding frustrated. 'This whore is the mother of every dealer, every son of a bitch, who deals here.'

'Maybe she really doesn't know,' I said.

'Hmm, maybe.'

'What did she say?' Kabir asked.

'That they don't kidnap people and everyone here is on their own will,' I said.

'That's not true.'

'I know.'

'What now?'

'I don't know,' I said.

My phone was ringing, it was Mr Kulkarni. I hoped he got some good news.

14.

'Are you sure she said she was here?' Inspector Joshi asked. He was the son in law of an old client of Priya's father. He was kind enough to reach the spot at two in the morning.

'Yes, this is what she said,' I said trying not to sound nervous.

'She left your place at half past nine, that is what you said, isn't it?' he asked Priya's grandma, who was standing numb and looking paralyzed.

'Yes,' she said in a broken accent.

'Was she tensed or worried about anything when she left?'

'No,' she said.

'Any other records after this?'

'After that, she called me but I missed the call,' I said.

'She called you again. Who are you?' he asked.

'I am Arijit,' I said and then realised what he actually meant, 'I mean I am her friend.'

'FRIEND? Tell me Arijit your every friend calls you twice in an hour?'

'No, but she called me for a reason,' I protested.

'And what is that?'

The Pragmatic

'She said she was feeling scared while she was passing the street and that is why she called.'

'Nothing else?'

'No.'

'Did you have a fight with her over the call?'

'No.'

'Sure?'

'Yes.'

'Anything else she mentioned?'

'Yes, she said she was passing through the other street but the strays dogs were having a fight there so she changed her route and reached here.'

'Mr Kulkarni,' he looked at him, 'who are these boys?'

'These are my friends. They came to help,' I said.

'So which places have you checked so far?'

We briefed him about the places and people we met so far. Michael said that they should go to the lady, *Akka*, as she might be knowing about her.

'How come you know a lot about this place?' he asked and looked at him with suspicious eyes.

'I draw portraits. I need models to pose for nude portraits. These are the cheapest ones so I come here frequently,' Michael said.

'Sounds convincing,' he said, 'Arijit, can I have a word with you, alone?'

'Sure,' I said and followed him.

'Is there anything you would like to add?'

'No, sir.'

'Was anyone among them present with you when you answered her call?'

'No. Sir let me make it clear, except Kabir no one amongst them has ever seen her. They are all Kabir's friends and they came here to help.'

'Okay. Any other suspicion?'

'No.'

'How is her family? How are her relations with her family?'

'Very good,' I said.

'So it is quite clear that she is either lost or kidnapped or met with an accident or something similar?'

'She can't be lost here. It's her city, she knows it as well as she knows her house.'

'Here they come,' he walked away as he saw a jeep full of uniformed officers arriving.

'We will be checking the whole area in as much detail as possible. And if you wish you can stay or it will be better if you take the ladies away from here,' he said to Mr Kulkarni.

'And you, the artist, can you show me the way to that lady's place?'

The Pragmatic

'Yeah, Sure,' Michael said.

'Others leave me your phone numbers on a piece of paper.'

'Can I have yours?' I asked him.

We exchanged numbers and then we were told to leave the place. And that they would call us when we would be needed, or when they will find us suspicious. Who knows?

Uncle stayed and I went to drop Priya's Grandma and mother at her house. It was nearly 3 am. As we stepped out of the Auto Rickshaw we saw that her place was crowded. Women, all in their night dresses, were gathered near the gate.

Ms Kulkarni started sobbing heavily as soon as she saw them. They tried to console her and her mother in law. All the men in her neighbourhood had begun searching different locations in the city. They searched for every possible route one can take from Priya's Grandma's place to her house.

Sun was just above the horizons. Everything outside the house was bright. Everything inside was still dark. Ms Kulkarni was still moaning and few of the women had stayed with her the whole night. No one slept, not even for a moment. Fifteen phone calls had been made to ask whether they found anything and every time the response was the same. Neighbours brought tea and breakfast for us. But Ms Kulkarni was in no mood of having anything. The ladies tried to make her understand that her fasting was not going to help them in finding her and she must have strength to cope up with the situation and must compose herself and what not.

Then one of the men came reporting that they had checked nearly all the places in the vicinity but with no good results. He also said that he knew someone from the local newspaper and advised that they should give a missing report in that newspaper.

Meanwhile, I messaged every number and group in my WhatsApp messenger and sent her photo informing them about the catastrophe and asking for any possible help.

Kabir had stayed at his friend's place as we were not supposed to go to the hostel. He brought a bike with him and came to pick me up. As soon as we reached the hostel, our fellow mates were all aware of what was going on and were enquiring whether we found her. I didn't want to talk about it and keep answering every stupid question that struck their evil little brains.

I unlocked my room's door and we entered.

'What are we going to do now?' Kabir Asked me.

'I don't know,' I said.

'Heard anything from her father?'

'No.'

'You shouldn't have done that.'

'What?' I asked.

'Informing everyone. She is a girl and being missing for a night is something she might not like everyone knowing about it,' he said.

The Pragmatic

'Well, you are right, but given the situation, I thought this is the most appropriate thing that could be done.'

My phone beeped as got a text from Sarang:

Msg me when u r back.

I replied saying that we were back. Within two minutes the door knocked.

He sat next to me and patted my back gently, 'everything will be perfectly fine,' he said.

I nodded trying not to shed tears in front of him.

Then he started inquiring about every detail. I explained him everything.

After thinking for a while he asked, 'she was having her phone with her?'

'Yes.'

'And the last person she called was you right?'

'Yes,' I was getting annoyed by these questions.

'Listen, my cousin works in an intelligence agency, we can ask him to trace the phone.'

'How can he trace a switched off phone?'

'At least he can trace where the phone was when just before it was turned off. Give me her number, I will ask him whether anything could be done.'

I gave him the number. He went outside talking with his cousin.

'Check the time when she called you,' he asked as he entered the room again about twenty minutes later.

'9.50 pm,' I said.

'And her phone was turned off at exact same time.'

It means that she was calling me when something went wrong. If not for my foolishness of not carrying my phone, in spite of knowing that she might call, things would have been very different.

'She didn't call you because she was scared again, this time she called you when she realised that something was wrong,' he said.

Kabir, who was sitting quietly for a while, suggested his hypothesis, 'this could be an accident.'

'How?' I asked.

'Imagine she is walking and trying to call you. Then suddenly she is struck by some vehicle, her phone falls down and breaks. Probably she might be in some hospital nearby, still unconscious.'

'But then people around there, whom you all inquired yesterday might have told you about that,' Sarang said.

'True,' he said and his hopeful expressions vanished.

I was still stuck in the thought that only if I had bothered to remember that she was going to call me, nothing of this sort would have happened.

15.

I waited for a very long time and assumed that they might have slept. There wasn't any noise from their room and the TV was turned off about an hour ago. I stood up from the bed feeling nervous. I slowly moved the door trying not to make the crinkling sound. I snooped into their room. The short guy was sleeping on the couch and the thin guy was sleeping on one of the iron beds at the other corner of the room.

I had two options. The first being to run straight away from the main door. But the door made a sound which was enough to wake up these drunk men. Other was to search for my sim card and call for help. I opted for the later one as it was less risky.

I walked very carefully looking out for my every step. There was complete silence and darkness, except for a small red bulb, in the room. I could clearly hear their breathing. I went near the DVD table and took a CD in my hand. Then I bent without touching anything in order to avoid any noise. I held the CD in my hand and pulled the sim card towards me. It came near, so I left the CD and reached the sim with my hand. I pulled it towards me, thinking that I made it.

As soon as I received the sim I almost cried. 'This can't be happening,' I thought. The sim card was broken in two pieces and this was just the half piece. I looked at the door and thought that if I ran away making some noise and they woke up, would they be able to catch me? The chances were less but if I get caught it was unimaginable what they will do with me and I will have to spend the rest of my life in this hell.

Suddenly I heard a voice from the couch. I slowly turned towards him and discovered that he was just snoring and that brought me some relief. But due to his snoring his phone caught my eye. I went near him and slowly lifted his phone and went back to my own room. I pressed the unlock button and hoped that it wouldn't be password protected. It wasn't. I looked at the time, it was 2.14 am.

I enabled data connection, enabled internet sharing over Wi-Fi. Then I turned on my phone and connected to his network. It got connected. Within few seconds I got hundreds of messages on my messenger. I ignored them. The question in front of me was how I could call anyone when even I didn't know what exactly my location was. I tried to remember where I ran when they started chasing me. I remembered the place but after that I was unconscious and had no idea where they took me. I tried to think of other options like calling the police and asking them to trace the location. The only problem was if I talked over the phone they would wake up and everything will end right away. Then suddenly, I remembered Aryan teaching me how to send our location using the WhatsApp messenger. I sent my location to everyone I knew in the city. I wrote 'I am here. Get me out fast' after the location. My phone's battery was about to die in about half an hour so I switched it off so that I might be able to use it in the morning when someone would see my message.

I went back to their room and placed his phone at the place where it earlier was, without making any noise. I came back to my room and sat on the bed. I imagined everything was going to be normal as it was earlier. I will be going to college, hanging around with Arijit and Kabir, coming home and annoying Aryan, getting scolded by

The Pragmatic

Aai for teasing him. Being Baba's little angel. I thought how worried they might be and, how much they might have suffered because of me as well as how much they are going to suffer.

Then suddenly I realised that things are not going to be same again. They couldn't be same again. I was no longer the same girl. These people had made me filthy, made me dirty. Even if I managed to get away from here, my suffering won't stop. It will begin in a new phase. I even thought of not going back home and being an embarrassment to my family. But that was out of the question for me. I can't live without my family. I know they will suffer in our society. People will never be the same for them and for me.

16.

We sat on a bench at the Senadatta police station. Inspector Joshi was inside the cabinet and we were asked to wait until he calls us for interrogation. The constable called out Kabir's name first. He looked nervous, really nervous.

'Why are you so tensed? They will just ask a few questions about you and maybe about where you came from and how do you know her and stuff. That's not a big deal. Chill,' I said. The inspector was already having a suspicion that someone from us was involved in the conspiracy to kidnap her. I feared that Kabir's nervousness might get him in some trouble.

'Past Arijit, past. My past may bring me some trouble,' he said and went inside.

After twenty long minutes he came outside and I was called in. His eyes were wet and he came out wiping them.

'What happened?'

He didn't say anything. Constable called my name again so I went inside.

'So Arijit, how long have you known each other?' Inspector asked.

'Four months. We met at my first day in college.'

'And how long have you been knowing Kabir?'

The Pragmatic

'I don't know why you are asking this.'

'Doesn't matter. Just answer.'

'Same, four months.'

'Tell me everything you know about Kabir.'

'Kabir? Why?' I asked him.

'I am the one who is supposed to ask questions here,' he said.

'Sir, if you are thinking that Kabir is involved in kidnapping her then let me tell you, three of us were, I mean are, we are best friends. He won't even imagine doing something like what you think.'

'Now will you please answer my question and let me do my work,' he said.

'Fine. But still I will protest the direction you are leading in,' I said 'I met Kabir when we were standing in a queue for buying the application form and prospectus for getting admission in the hostel. His father was the one who initiated the conversation.

He asked everything about filling the form to me as he was poor in English. Even though Kabir understood English and was filling the form properly, his father ignored him and followed my instructions. Which was a bit strange. After this incident, we met during our first day. At first, I found him a very stupid boy but later it turned out that he was just easy going and was very wise. He lacked academic intelligence but is very active socially.'

'That's it?' he asked after I stopped.

'Yes, sir.'

'You didn't mention about his illness,' He frowned.

'Illness? I didn't get you.'

'Don't act smart. You know what I am talking about.' he said and came closer to my chair.

I got scared as he stood only a few inches away from me.

'No, I don't,' I said.

'If I figured out that you are lying to me,' he brought his face near mine, 'it's going to be bad for you,' I could feel his breath as he said this.

He moved away and grabbed his seat again.

'Do you know he is two years older than you?'

'No,' I said.

'Do you know he is mentally sick?'

'What do you mean by that?'

'He was in a mental hospital for a while. He tried to escape from there twice but failed each time. He can see people who don't exist.'

I was in shock at this point and was unable to say a word.

'How do you know all these?' I asked thinking that the inspector is trying some trick on me.

'His friends told me. They were here before you two came. When I asked Kabir whether anything was wrong with him,

The Pragmatic

he didn't say anything. When I told him that I know everything about him, he started to cry. He had not accepted that he was involved, but my eyes are on him.'

'Can I go?' I asked.

'Sure.'

I stood up with lots of questions in my mind.

'Strange, isn't it?' inspector Joshi asked as I reached the door.

'What?' I turned facing him.

'You were calling him your best friend and you hardly even know about him. Many times mentally sick people, unwillingly, commit some crime just to take revenge for small acts or even to gain attention. You keep an eye on him and inform me immediately if you find anything suspicious about him.'

I nodded.

Outside, I saw Kabir lost in his thoughts, his eyes still red.

'Kabir,' I said. 'We need to talk.'

We walked out of the police station and were standing at the bus stop. Neither of us had said anything. It was Kabir who broke the silence, 'you want to ask something?'

'Shall I ask or you can read my mind?' I said not looking towards him.

'I just... J-U-S-T didn't want to lose you two. I don't want you to freak out after knowing that I am mentally sick.'

'You don't trust us?' I asked, this time, looking straight into his eyes.

'I have no trust on my fate. Look, shit happened again. Shit has happened every time. When I was in school. When I was in the hospital. When I was in a mental rehabilitation centre. When I was in junior college. I thought I had escaped the misfortune of my life but see again it surfaced and slapped on my face from front.'

We both looked away. A silence followed. Impatient silence. Then the bus arrived and we went inside.

'Don't judge me by whatever that has happened. It should not have happened this way, in the middle of all this,' he said almost to himself. He looked away and wiped the tear that was flowing down his right cheek.

'I am not judging you,' I said, 'but…'

'I know. But given the circumstances, you have a right to judge me in any way you want. But let me have my word of defence before you conclude anything.'

'Sure, you can. I want to know everything.'

'Even though I am not NORMAL and I, apparently, don't like Priya much but that doesn't mean that I could do something like what the inspector is claiming. I swear. Not even in my dream I could think of something like that.'

He paused. He sighed.

'Anyone does it or not, I want you of all people to believe me. I care for her as I care for you and I will kill myself before thinking of doing something like this.'

'I know,' I said.

The Pragmatic

'You know what?'

'That you won't do anything like this. I want to know why you lied to us about you.'

'I told you I don't want you to judge me as a mentally sick person. I cannot afford to lose more friends and become isolated again. I just can't. I never imagined that I have to tell you about this, but my fate, it has always ditched me. Same goes for this time.' He started to cry like a child. My thoughts shifted back to Priya.

'Kabir, for now, let's leave it the way it is. I believe that you are in no way involved and I will need a clear justification and an honest word about you later. But I think it is more important to focus on the fact that two days have passed since Priya is missing and we have to do something to find her,' I said.

The fact that two days had pass was devastating. It was killing me. I avoided to think about any negative thing that might have happened to her. Whenever any such thought struck my mind I found myself helpless and weeping. So I avoided such thoughts.

We reached our hostel and Kabir had stopped crying. It was the first time I saw him crying.

I took my bag and locked the door. Kabir was in time. Since yesterday he was behaving a little odd. We were going to meet Priya's parents.

Meanwhile, every student in college came to know about the tragic incident and was willing to help in every possible way. Pamphlets, bearing her photo and contact numbers were distributed and an appeal to help to find the girl was made in a local newspaper, the one for which her mother wrote articles. The people in her neighbourhood were wandering in the city continuously, dividing the city into different sections and assigning sections to a group of individuals. Everything possible was being done with no fruitful results. It was the third day and hopes were getting down.

We reached her home. No one was in the hall so we went straight to the bedroom where her parents, her Grandma and Aryan were sitting. All of them had dark circles around their eyes and all looked sick. Her father was talking to someone over the phone giving details about what happened that night. Her mother was sitting numb and her grandma was trying to feed Aryan who didn't seem interested in eating. His eyes were dark red, probably because of crying.

We folded our legs and sat on the ground. I didn't know what to say or what to ask so I just kept quiet. The silence was unbearable. The condition of her family was very unpleasant. Her mother began to cry again. She seemed to have lost weight and looked like she was suffering from some deadly disease. Her father walked away still talking on the phone.

Aryan walked towards the door and asked me to follow him. I walked towards him, he held my hand and took me in his room which he shared with Priya. He opened his school bag and took out something which looked like some greeting card kept in an envelope.

The Pragmatic

'Hmm,' he said, 'take this.'

'What is it?' I asked and I noticed my name written on the left top corner of the envelope.

'I stole from her bag to tease her when she went out that night. It bears your name so I thought I could tease her and blackmail her that I will show this to *baba*,' he said and fell silent, 'but she didn't return,' he broke into tears. I went close to him and held him. I wiped his tears and said that she would be back soon. That everyone was searching for her, even the police officers, so we would definitely find her.

'I know,' he said.

I looked at the envelope and thought it was an inappropriate time to open this. So I put it in my bag and went to the other room. As I sat on the floor Kabir gestured his hands asking what happened.

'Nothing,' I said.

I remember she had mentioned about a letter she was about to gift me. This might be the same letter, I thought.

17.

I was lying on the bed. Another vigil night. I was thinking about where and how she might be. I had hardly slept in last three days. Every time I tried to rest, some creepy thought entered my mind. I once dreamed of her being kidnapped and moved away in another city and people keeping her locked in a room and doing unimaginable things. All such thoughts were scary but somewhere I knew they were not far away from being a probable explanation.

'Arijit, Arijit,' Kabir shouted banging the door loudly, 'open this door, quick, it's about Priya.'

I got up quickly and opened the door. He showed me his phone. He had received a message from Priya along with her location, from her own number. I dialled her number but it was switched off.

'You replied her? Did she reply back?' I asked.

'I tried sending her a message. When I was typing she was online, as soon I sent the message she went offline. She hadn't received my messages. But now we have the location, let's move.'

I called Inspector Joshi and asked Kabir to lock my room.

'Hello, who is this?' he asked in a sleepy voice.

'Arijit, sir. Priya's friend.'

The Pragmatic

'Priya? The missing girl?' he asked.

'Yes sir, she managed to send us her location. I forwarded you the message, it's in the same area where she was lost.'

'Okay. Are you sure about it?'

'Hundred percent sure, sir. The message is sent by her own number,' I added.

'I will be there. Don't do anything before we arrive. I am saying again don't try to be a hero. This is a police affair you stay as far as possible. Is it clear?'

'Yes, it is,' I said.

'Good,' he ended the call.

Now we have to leave the hostel block. There was no one on the block's gate and it was locked. I quickly ran towards the point where the third and fourth block met. The two hostel blocks were two rectangles with a common vertex. At their point of intersection, there was a gap and a small wall was constructed there. I climbed the wall and jumped on the other side. Kabir followed me. But he fell on his nose and it started bleeding.

'Are you okay?' I asked.

'Yes,' he said and stood up.

Now the main gate was still there to be crossed. No watchmen were around so there was no question of unlocking it. We went near the gate. It was made of vertical metal rods welded together. One of the rods was missing. I passed through the rod easily. Kabir, due to his oversized physique, was having trouble and after a certain point was not able to move further.

I heard someone whistling at us, he held a torch and was running towards us whistling louder. He came near and stopped. He was Manoj mama, one of our watchmen.

'Mama it's an emergency, please don't stop us,' I begged.

'Is it about that girl whose photo you put on the notice board?' he asked.

'Yes, mama. We got to know where she is and we have to reach there as soon as possible,' Kabir said struggling between the metal rods.

He unlocked the door and he even gave us the key to his bike.

―――

Kabir was driving the bike as we headed towards the location.

I called Mr Kulkarni.

'Hello,' he said in a dizzy voice.

'Uncle, Priya messaged her location. She is near the place we met that day.'

'OH MY GOD! I will be there, OH MY GOD,' he said.

'I have informed the Inspector. He will be reaching their shortly,' I said and wondered whether he was listening. I could hear him telling others that we had found her location.

'Thank you, son, I will inform the police now. Bye,' he said and ended the call.

The Pragmatic

'Kabir, can't you drive faster?' I said looking into the map on my phone. Her location was in the red light area, which wasn't a pleasant news.

'Chill man, Chill. We are just ten minutes away,' he said.

We were the first ones to reach there, followed by her parents. We decided to hide before the police arrive as we didn't want to catch anyone's attention.

'This building, isn't it?' uncle asked.

'No. You are not holding it properly,' I said and turned his phone upside down, 'look, it's the opposite one.'

It was the building in which we had met *Akka*. It meant she had lied to us. It meant she knew that day about Priya being there. I was very impatiently waiting for police to arrive. Mr Kulkarni, on the other hand, was asking to go in the building and kick the bastards on their asses.

'What if they have weapons?' I asked trying to stop him, 'one wrong move and we will lose everything.'

'You are right. But they might be doing something wrong with my girl right there, right now,' he pointed towards the building, 'and I am standing here doing nothing but waiting for help to arrive. This is very difficult for me son.'

I didn't say anything. I just wanted him to stay quiet until the police arrive.

'This is not the time to be aggressive. This is the time to be patient, uncle,' Kabir said.

He seemed to be convinced with what Kabir said as he kept quiet. Fortunately, the police van arrived soon. They stopped at some distance. Only the Inspector came out. He saw us and walked towards us.

'This building, isn't it?' he asked pointing towards to the building at the opposite side.

'No, it's that one,' uncle said pointing towards the building I had shown him.

'This is the place where *Akka* lives,' inspector said looking at the building, 'you all will stay here until we return with her.' It was wonderful to think that I will be able to see her again in a couple of minutes.

Inspector looked at his van and nodded as three other men in uniform came out of the van and followed him as he went inside. We waited there holding our breaths. I felt uncle holding my hand firmly and nervously. We all were looking at the building in unison. He released my hand and began praying.

After ten minutes I saw them coming out of the building with a girl, two other men, and *Akka*. I looked at the girl, she wasn't Priya. The officers took the two men and *Akka* with them in the van. My eyes were still fixed on the entrance. I was hoping to see her come out. But no one came out.

The Inspector came near us holding the girl. Her hair were totally messed up, she looked like she was beaten up heavily and there was a mark of dried blood on the left edge of her lip. And when he came closer I looked carefully at the girl. She was Priya. Her condition was horrible and I wasn't the only one who didn't recognise her. Her face had become grimly dark, her right cheekbone was surfaced with a big open scar and lips were swollen. She had lost a considerable amount of weight and was dressed in the most pathetic manner. She was in a semi-conscious state. The inspector advised that she should be taken to a hospital immediately and we headed to the nearest one.

18.

I was staring at the wall in front of me. The bright colour in addition with the yellow tungsten bulb was again annoying me. I moved back and rested my back on the wall behind and folded my legs bringing my knees close to my chest. I looked around for something but didn't understand what I was looking for. I felt upset not finding it. The door made a crinkling sound again and I looked at the door in horror. The two demons entered with liquor bottles in their hands.

I brought my legs closer to me and started to breathe heavily. I was terrified.

'Please, not again,' I begged knowing that my begging will not have any effect on this heartless bastards.

One of them laughed at my begging as he sipped liquor from his bottle. He seemed to enjoy that I, girl, was begging helplessly in front of him and that this somehow made him powerful.

'I will run away,' I said, 'and will make sure you two are caught by police. My dad is an advocate and he will take care of the rest.' I tried to threaten them but that was of no use. They didn't seem to pay any attention to whatever I was saying.

'Do you think we are scared of police? Not to mention a bloody advocate,' the first guy said.

'And, even if you managed to run away from here, believe me, I will make sure we get you back here. No one will be able to stop us *from doing so. And where will you run? Your home! Huh! Don't you think that's a stupid idea? If we can kidnap you once, surely we can kidnap you again. Wherever you go, wherever you hide, we will be there.'* He said as he kept his bottle on the table and came on the bed. I kicked him protesting but the other one took hold of me. Then I tried kicking harder and harder.

My eyes were closed when I was trying to push him away. I opened my eyes to realise that it was my mother's hand which was grabbing me and I was kicking on the bed I was lying. I looked around, the place looked like a hospital room. Baba came running from outside accompanied by a few others. But I only saw him coming close to me and hugging me. He had tears in his eyes and was sobbing. Surprisingly, I found no tears in my eyes. I was stunned. He asked me how I was feeling. I had nothing to say. I was too disturbed to utter anything. I looked around to see whether the two demons were hiding somewhere around. I told him to check around for them. He assured that no one was around and they were arrested. But I was not convinced.

'They will come to get me,' I said, 'I know they will. Get them arrested Baba, please get them or else they will be here anytime. They are very dangerous Baba.'

'They are already arrested. Don't worry no one can do any harm to you now,' he said.

I kept quiet. But I knew that they will come and get me when no one is around.

19.

'She was screaming and crying like hell,' I said. I was sitting in Sarang's room. Three days had passed since Priya got her first trauma attack in the hospital. And after that such attacks were regular in a course of few hours.

'Well, that is pretty obvious. We can't even imagine what she might be going through,' he said.

Then I fell silent for a moment. Things were getting very difficult and I came to him with some hope of getting out of the depression in which I was sinking. But he was, as usual, acting very differently from what I expected.

'I was about to visit you,' he said after the pause, 'I am going home tomorrow to collect some documents.'

I gave him a blank expression.

'And I want you to join me,' he added.

'Why? No, bhaiya, I don't think I can come,' I said.

'There is something I want you to know about.'

'You can tell me here.'

'No. I want you to meet someone,' he said 'and the rest is up to you.'

'What rest?' I asked to which he didn't bother to answer.

'I cannot force you but I really want you to come with me.'

———

Sarang's native place was in Shirur taluka, in Pune district itself, an hour's journey away from the city area. We were on his bike and he was saying a few things about his village. He also mentioned that we were going to his aunt's place first and then we will continue our journey. And slowly I was getting why he wanted me to come along. This journey was making me feel better. I hadn't visited any place, not even in our hostel's vicinity since the incident occurred. I thought he felt that I needed some energy to be strong enough to be on her side and hence he brought me. I also thought to ask Priya's father to take her away for a while so that she might feel somewhat better and this could lessen her trauma.

We waited at a railway crossing and I looked towards my right horizon to check why it was taking so much time for the train to arrive.

'How much time it will take for us to meet your aunt?' I asked, just for the sake of asking something to break the silence.

'We are not going to meet my aunt. We are going to visit her house.'

'And how are these two things different?'

'She doesn't live with her family. She lives at my father's house,' he said and the train was visible now.

I was not sure about asking any more questions. This was quite a family issue so I thought of not pushing him any further.

'Ask,' he said as if he was reading my mind.

'Why are we going to her place then?' I asked.

'To meet her husband, my uncle. I told you I wanted you to meet someone. Uncle is that someone.'

'Are they divorced?' I asked, still thinking that I was asking too personal questions to him.

'No,' he answered.

'Then?'

'Then what?'

'Nothing,' I said looking at the bogies in front of me. The noise of the train made it difficult for us to continue our talk, much to my relief. But a part of me was still curious about them.

———

His uncle's house was a typical village house. Huge in size, spacious, surrounded by plants and a huge banyan tree in the right corner and a large tractor parked near the tree. He was sitting on a wooden chair and was having his evening tea when he saw us. An expression of surprise on his face was visible when he saw us. Sarang went near him, touched his feet and got his blessings. I was wondering why he wanted me to meet this man, who was looking completely normal except the way he was surprised to see us.

The Pragmatic

Two children came out with chairs. Uncle introduced me to both of them and asked the elder one, who must be sixteen, to prepare tea for us.

'What brings you here?' he asked.

'I was going home, thought to have a look at Shrish's studies. His board exams are approaching, aren't they?'

'Yeah. And I think he will score decent marks,' he paused then continued, 'he would have studied much better but he is very much busy in household chores and parenting his younger brother. I wished I could afford to keep a maid.'

Meanwhile, Shirish came out of the kitchen with five cups of tea and few biscuits for all of us.

'Prepared for the boards, champ?' Sarang asked him.

He didn't answer. He was looking downwards and grief was visible on his face. He placed the tray on the table and ran inside weeping.

No one said anything. An intense silence followed. Sarang stood up and went inside. Uncle took a sip of tea. His eyes were wet and he was trying to avoid any eye contact with me. Probably because he didn't want me to see his tearful eyes.

I didn't know what to say or what not to say. So I kept quiet and took a sip of my tea. But then I thought it was insensitive of me not to ask him anything. I kept my cup and started to think of something that may divert his mind.

'Did you watch yesterday's match?' I asked realising it wasn't the best question to be asked at that moment. And he didn't say a word. He slowly lifted his hand and removed his specs with one hand and wiped his eyes with the other one.

I wanted to ask him why he was crying. I wanted to console him. But I sat there frozen without any idea of what was happening. I stood up and went inside so that he may cry without being conscious of someone staring at him. Crying is one of the gifts bestowed upon humans.

Inside, I saw Sarang sitting on a bed with Shirish resting his head on his lap.

'She asks about me?' Shirish asked.

'Yes. Every day,' he said.

'Then why is she not coming here to see us?'

Sarang fell silent and Shirish realised that his mother didn't ask about him every day.

'Has she forgotten me?' he asked.

'No. She just needs some time.'

'How much? I haven't talked to her for four years and haven't seen her for two years,' he burst into tears again.

Sarang was quiet now. He was just moving his palm over Shirish's head and trying to console him. Uncle came inside with Shirish's younger brother Nitesh. Nitesh must be around ten and he too was crying. I had started feeling guilty for coming here and making them all cry.

Uncle came close to Shirish and sat on the floor next to the bed. Shirish stood up and came closer to his father, rested his head on his shoulder and began to weep. I could see that

The Pragmatic

uncle was fighting hard to control his tears. He was a grown up man and this was his biggest weakness, he was not supposed to cry, at least, not in front of his sixteen and ten years old children.

Sarang was riding his bike and I was sitting behind him still shocked with what just happened a couple of minutes earlier and wondering whether I should ask about it or wait till he talks himself.

'Ask,' he said, again reading my mind.

'What was that?' I asked. 'What happened with your aunt?'

'Wait a minute,' he said and parked his bike near a tea stall.

We sat there and ordered tea.

He began, 'my aunt and uncle married eighteen years ago. This was one of the first love marriages in their village and obviously, the community was against it. My grandfather was in their favour but uncle's father didn't want his son to marry my aunt as they were Brahmins and my aunt wasn't.'

He took a sip from his cup and continued, 'they decided to go against his father and got married with blessings of my Grandfather. As expected aunt's father in law was so outraged with the scandalous behaviour of his son that he kicked him out of his home. So they settled in a different village, with some help from my grandfather, which you just saw.'

Happy ending, isn't it? But after some years my aunt gave birth to Shirish and a few years later Nitesh was born.

Uncle's father's heart finally melted when he saw his grandchildren and welcomed Uncle and his family to live with them. They were delighted and immediately joined their family. Everyone was happy except Shirish's elder uncle who was not allowed to marry a girl of his choice and was instead forcefully married to a woman who eventually left him alone with his carnal desires unfulfilled.

Once when my uncle was out with his father and children were at my place. The sadist used that opportunity and along with his two friends gang raped my aunt.'

―――

We reached his house. It was a huge house with a lot of open space surrounding it. Three cars were parked in the parking area and adjacent to it was a well, equipped with machinery to pull out water from it. Two large coconut trees were standing next to the well giving the whole scene an artistic look. The sun was about to set and the surrounding light had turned dark yellowish red.

His mother came out listening to the sound of the bike. We went inside and were ordered to wash our hands and legs only after which we were allowed to eat or drink anything. We sat on the chairs as his father, Mr Shitole, joined us. His mother brought some snacks and drinks and asked him why had he became so thin and weren't the people in his mess providing him with proper food. I looked around for his aunt but she was nowhere. His family started their chat about that year's rain problems, their farming, about the village politics, about his studies and future plans.

'How is *Atya*', he asked referring to his aunt. This caught my attention.

The Pragmatic

'She is fine. No improvements yet,' Mr Shitole sadly said, 'how is the climate in Pune?' he asked trying to change the topic as I was present there.

'It's very cold there,' I said.

'Are you in *Sonu's* class?' Mrs Shitole asked.

'No. I am in the first year now. He is two years senior to me. We are in the same hostel block.'

'I will show him our house,' Sarang said and stood up picking a handful of snacks.

We went into his room first and he showed me his huge collection of books and games. At that moment I wasn't interested in any of that.

'Where is your aunt? I am here to meet her, right?'

'Yeah. But I will have to ask my dad first.'

―――

It was not difficult to say how beautiful she would look if her face was washed and her hair were combed. Apparently no one, including her, bothered about her appearances anymore. She wore a plain brown gown and was sitting still on her bed with her knees folded to her breasts. She didn't notice us as we entered or maybe she noticed and didn't respond.

I stood at one corner of the room and watched Sarang as he went near her bed.

'When did you come?' she asked in a monotonous voice, looking away from him.

'An hour ago. How are you feeling now?'

She sighed and laughed sarcastically, 'the therapist says that I will be normal again if I listened to him. Even magic cannot make things normal again. Tell your dad not to waste money on that therapist.'

Her eyes were beautiful and at the same time were reflecting her grief and pain. According to her, she had lost her soul, those men have made her body dirty and filthy. She once said that she didn't have the courage to end her life by herself. She even asked doctors to do so but they refused.

'You will be fine *Atya*,' he said and stood up to leave. She nodded and pressed her face inside her knees. I followed him out.

20.

I was lying on a mat on the terrace. We were in their old house which was half a kilometre away from their current one. The cold was unbearable. Sarang said he will be back with sweaters but was taking a long time to return. Meanwhile, I was looking at the stars and I realised Dan Brown was so right when, in his book *The last Symbol*, he wrote that we are a very different person when we lie down just looking at the night sky. My thoughts were still somewhere in between Priya and the lady I met today. I rubbed my hands in order to generate some heat.

He came with a pair of sweaters in one of his hands and a diary in the other hand.

'Sky is pretty clear from here, isn't it?' he asked.

'It's marvellous!' I said, 'can you see that Orion nebula in the Orion constellation?' I pointed towards the constellation, 'It is never visible from our city.'

'I know,' he said and sat down, 'but certainly, we are not here to talk about constellations.'

'Yeah.'

He then took out a cigarette packet from his pocket. He held one cigarette in between his lips and offered me one.

'Have you ever smoked earlier?' he asked.

I didn't say anything and took the cigarette from his hand. Trying to follow him I too held the cigarette in between my lips. He lighted them and offered the lighter to me. I brought the flame near my cigarette and tried to lit it up.

'Inhale. You got to inhale.'

I did as he said and inhaled some smoke while lighting the cigarette. I coughed and handed the lighter to him.

'You sure you wanna try?'

'Yes,' I said. I took another puff and coughed again. It felt exactly like passive smoking.

'Swallow the smoke. Let it go inside you,' he said.

I took a puff again and swallowed the smoke. I felt warmth in my windpipe as the smoke moved inside. I then slowly exhaled it through my mouth. Damn! it felt good.

'Shall we continue?' I asked.

'Sure. After the calamity, *Atya* didn't speak anything for a week. She was in shock. Uncle took her to a psychiatrist who said that either she will heal with time or she will remain in this state for her entire life. Uncle left his father's home after the incident and came back to his old house. He was without money so he was not able to afford to take her to better hospitals. Six months passed and all he had was hope that she will one day wake up on her own and prepare breakfast for the children. But the day never came. She used to sit in her room not talking to anyone, not even to her children, the whole day. She didn't cry either. She was too traumatised to cry.

The Pragmatic

A year passed and she showed no signs of improvement. But my uncle is a very patient and loving husband. He stood by her side. He played the role of a good father as well as a good mother for his children. At the same time, he was always there playing the role of an ideal husband. But all his efforts were apparently in vain. The more he tried getting close to her the more disappointed he became. Once he held her hand and she shouted screaming for help. When the neighbours came she complained that the man was trying to rape, only later she realised that the man was her own husband.'

The temperature was falling rapidly, he rubbed his hand and looked away. I was looking at him without blinking my eyes. I was waiting impatiently for him to resume the story.

'Have you understood what I am trying to say?' he asked.

'Not exactly. But I will appreciate if you finished this story first and then we can talk,' I said.

'As you say. After few days *Baba* visited her and told uncle that he wanted to take her to a therapist, about whom he had heard a lot from his friend. He wanted to give it another try. Uncle agreed. *Baba* also said that he wanted her to stay with us till the treatment is completed as my *Aai* will be there to take her proper care. Uncle agreed to that as well. He knew it was for her betterment. Every possible treatment was done. Many psychiatrists and therapists were consulted but with no success.

'The real difficult times were when her children asked about their mother. Uncle was left alone to deal with their upbringing and their questions for which he didn't have any answers. My uncle was a very strong person and a very loving husband but eventually he lost his patience and this started to deteriorate his peaceful nature. He was emotionally broken. My aunt is alive. But she is just a living body. She is not the person I knew. Not the person my uncle loved. Those bastards have killed the soul of my aunt and now what remains is just her body.'

He sighed.

'And...' he hesitated.

'And what?'

'And I don't want you to be like my uncle.' A painful silence followed as I understood what this all was about.

'He could have married. He still can but he refuses to do so. He still has false hopes that she will regain herself. Four years have passed and I haven't seen him smiling. Not even once. Every time we talk about her, he comes up with a reason blaming himself for what happened. He can move on which will guarantee a better life for him and for his children. But he chooses to wait.'

I was lost in my own thoughts. I didn't notice he had stopped talking. I wanted to go to bed. Another thoughtful and vigil night was waiting for me.

> *Some Relations you break, some break you;*
> *Some Decisions you make, some make you.*

This was the second verse from his incomplete poem whose first verse he had shared with me on my birthday. He showed me this verse from his diary just before we left the

The Pragmatic

terrace and I went straight to the bedroom in their current house where I was supposed to sleep. But sleep was a very expensive luxury.

'Polite distance,' was the term he used implying to stay away from her for my own benefit. I admit she is a completely different person now. She is no more the girl I know, the girl I loved. And after knowing his aunt I doubted to meet that girl. But I just couldn't leave her in such tragic circumstances. She was in need of support, especially emotional support. But again, as he said, I didn't want to end up like his uncle. I didn't want to imagine myself in his place. But then again when I thought of Priya, I wanted to be at her side. Holding her hand, consoling her, convincing her that eventually, everything will be fine again. But was everything going to be fine again?

I woke up and stepped out of the room. I looked at the wall clock. It was 11 am. We were supposed to leave at 10 am.

'Good morning,' Sarang said. He was dressed and ready to leave, 'make it quick.'

'Yes,' I said and yawned. 'Give me fifteen minutes.'

I took my stuff and went for a quick bath. After undressing I turned the shower nob slowly to check the temperature of water. Even at 11 am the water was pretty cold. I stepped back and the turned the nob to its full extent. The water started gushing out. I moved my right leg and as soon as the water touched my skin I pulled my leg away from the stream. It was very cold. On a count of three, I entered the streams of cold water and felt how it embraced my body. But it wasn't cold anymore. My body had adapted to the cold and now was a part of it. Now stepping out of this waterfall would cause discomfort.

Any new thought that entered my mind was not always welcomed. But when I gently forced my mind, it made its way. The thought was then felt throughout my body and was soon a part of my being. And then it was embraced by the mind to such an extent that life without it seemed somewhat different, somewhat difficult.

―――

I was back in my room and Kabir wanted to know why Sarang asked me to go along with him. I explained him every detail and was waiting for his response. But he was quiet and neutral with his expressions.

'So?' he asked looking straight into my eyes. I avoided an eye contact and stayed quiet pretending to think.

'So what?' I asked just in order to break the uncomfortable silence.

'She needs you,' he said and I felt something heavy in my lungs.

'I know,' I paused, 'I know,' I said and held my face in my palms.

'I thought you didn't like her,' I said knowing that it may sound stupid but I was trying to convince him that I was not being selfish. I was just being practical.

'You are right, I never really liked her. Do yo…' he was about to add something when I interrupted him.

The Pragmatic

'Then why do you want me to be with her?' I asked.

'Will you let me complete my sentence?' he said, 'I never liked her. But do you know why?'

'No, I don't.'

'Because my best friend is no longer my friend when he is with her,' he said. 'He doesn't bother to listen to me or pay any attention. I don't exist for you when she is around. The worst part is that she is a deserving person. A charming, intelligent and *your type* so there aren't any hopes that my friend will be only my best friend again. That leaves me with no other option than not liking her.'

I was quiet.

'What are you up to?' I asked.

'What are YOU up to?' he asked. His voice was getting louder, 'I see where this is going. If you think that after being raped she is no more eligible for…'

'I never said that,' I said.

'To hell with what you said, to hell with what that bastard had fed in your evil little brain,' he was sounding scary. 'If you are going to leave her, believe me, I will rape you and make sure that you both are on the same page.'

'And who are you to teach me? A psychic boy who hears the voices that don't even exist. Who is supposed to be in a mental hospital but is free because he lies to everyone that he is fine.'

He stared at me. I was able to feel the terror inside me due to his wrath. He stood up to leave.

'Fuck you Arijit,' he said and left.

I knew I shouldn't have said that. I screwed up once again.

21.

Knock-Knock.

'Who?' Kabir said.

'It's me. Arijit'

'What do you want?'

'You.'

'Busy.'

'Shut up and open the door.'

He opened the door and without looking at me went inside and sat on the bed looking at the window.

'Look,' I said. 'You know I didn't mean it.'

'No. I don't,' he said.

'Pardon.'

'How would I know you meant it or not?'

'Okay. I am sorry. I was confused and stressed and anxious…'

'And disgusting,' he said.

'Yes. Disgusting.'

'And stupid.'

'Okay, stupid.'

'And dumb.'

'Enough now,' I said.

'Just one more. Dumb. You are dumb.'

'Stop now,' I said in a serious tone.

'Arijit, don't let anyone play with your mind and manipulate your decisions,' he said.

'I am not letting him manipulate me. But what he said made sense.'

'Now look at this. There is a boy. There is a girl. They fell in love. The girl is raped. The boy leaves her. Does it make sense?'

'You are right Kabir but still I cannot imagine my future with her anymore. Not in the condition she is in right now.'

'She needs you Arijit. You should be at her side now. At least for now.'

'I will be at her side. I will be,' I said mostly convincing myself.

'I am going to her place today. You want to come along?'

'Not today. Maybe tomorrow,' I said and left the room.

———

'How is she?' I asked as we walked on our way back from the mess.

'Go and ask her yourself.'

I sighed.

'You're too much.'

'I am too much? Really?'

'Do you want to start again?'

'No.'

'Then tell me how is she?'

'Not fine. She is getting her trauma attacks twice or thrice every day. She is not able to talk to anyone except her parents. Not even with me. I talked with her for few minutes. Asking casual questions, which she answered properly but then she was very uncomfortable. Moreover, she has this strange feeling of guilt inside her as if she is responsible for what had happened.'

'Guilt?' I asked.

'Yes. She keeps on apologizing about going to the place. She has done this several times. She also thinks that she is bringing shame to her family's reputation.'

'What the hell!' I said.

We reached our block.

'I will be glad if you come along with me tomorrow.'

I paused for a second, 'sure. Let's go tomorrow.'

I was feeling nervous to face her. I haven't visited her since the day she was discharged from the hospital. Kabir told me that she never asked about me. Which was in some way quite a relief. Mr Kulkarni was sitting on the couch in the hall with a sad face. He saw us and stood up. I looked at him and felt sorry for him.

'Hello son. How are you? Where have you been?' he asked.

'I went home and was there for the last few days,' I lied, 'Priya is in her room?'

'Yes,' he said as we headed towards her room.

'Is she better now?'

'Huh,' he sighed. 'No. She is getting worse,' he said.

I thought it will be better if I didn't ask further questions.

She was sleeping when we entered. Mr Kulkarni woke her up. She wasn't sleeping. Just pretending to sleep. As soon as he called her name she turned herself away and folded her knees close to her torso. I wondered whether we should wake her or not.

'Look your friends are here,' Mr Kulkarni said trying to sound as optimistic as possible.

She didn't move. Neither said a word.

'We can come later,' I said.

'Let's sit in the hall. We will return when her mother is here,' he said and we headed back to the hall, 'she is quite comfortable when her mother is around.'

We sat on the couch and in the next half an hour heard about the suggestion their relatives and neighbours were offering.

The Pragmatic

Like they should leave the city and move where Mr Kulkarni worked when he was young; they should get her married as quickly as possible or they should take her to some hypnotherapist, God knows why. One man even suggested to call a Brahmin and get her body purified by some rituals which would make her mind free again.

'What about the culprits? What are the actions taken against them?' I asked. Kabir has earlier mentioned that the case is being postponed because Priya's word may have a profound effect on the Judge's decision. They were waiting for her to get better.

Then her father started to narrate the whole scenario including what happened that day and how the culprits were falsely blaming her.

―――

Jaykant Surve was the grandson of Mr Manohar Surve, ex-MP. Besides being a shame to his family, Jaykant was an elite customer of Rafiz and Dinesh.

Rafiz was thirteen and Dinesh was slightly younger when both did the job of collecting recyclable goods from municipality garbage bins and exchanging them for money with which they used to buy bread. One day a lady, unusual in her looks, asked them if they would like to work for her. She promised them food and shelter in return. She never mentioned her name but people in her vicinity called her *Akka*.

Now Jaykant or Jaya paid them three times of what other customers paid. So the duo always made it a point never to disappoint Jaya. Their relation had become stronger and Jaya spent so much money on the duo that they were ready to do anything for him, even if it meant kidnapping an innocent girl, which *Akka* never allowed them, so that Jaya may fulfil his carnal desires.

Priya was, unfortunately, this innocent girl who happened to be present at the wrong place at the wrong time. When she passed in front of Jaya, his lustful eyes immediately got glued to her. He signalled Rafiz, who was hesitant, but was not in a position to decline Jaya's order. He followed his order and quietly followed Priya. Priya, who was walking faster now due to a suspicion of someone following her, tried to make a call but the person she was trying to reach, me, was not answering her call. She slipped her phone into her jeans pocket and started to run. Suddenly Dinesh appeared out of the blues and Rafiz signalled him to catch her. He blocked her way and grabbed her hand. Then both Jaya and Rafiz came running and they together made her unconscious and lifted her, heading towards the place where she was about to be kept for the next few days.

Priya narrated them the story from the part where she was being followed. But that was the day when she was quite good, at least better than other days. Also, she was alone with him when she said all these. She didn't say a word about what happened after this.

And when she was asked to give a statement in front of the inspector, her lips didn't utter a word.

Jaya's advocate, on the other hand, made a counter argument that she was the one who willingly offered herself to Rafiz and after getting scared of all the happenings there, she made up the story. Now, without her statement, it was

The Pragmatic

difficult to prove them guilty. And she was not in a position to make a statement in front of anyone. After that incident, she was not able to talk about it in even in front of her father. Besides her therapist was advising that she should not be reminded of the incident again and again as it makes her mental condition worse. It was decided that when she was healthy enough to make a statement then and only then this topic will be raised again. Till then the culprits were released on bail.

Having narrated the incident and the details, Mr Kulkarni fell silent. Both of us had no idea what to say.

'She will be fine, uncle. You are here, aunty is here and we all are here,' Kabir said.

'Hopefully. Son, hopefully,' he said as he removed his spectacles and rubbed his eyes with his fingers.

A strange current of guilt ran throughout my body as I looked in her eyes. Our eyes met for a brief moment and immediately she looked away. She sat resting her back on the wall. Her half body was covered with a blanket. Hair messed up, cheek bones bulging outwards, dark circles and weight loss altogether made her look miserable.

'How are you feeling now?' I asked as I sat on the chair next to her bed.

'Fine,' she said.

A silence followed. Uneasy and uncomfortable.

'You had your lunch?' I asked.

She nodded.

'She eats for namesake. She is ruining her appetite by refusing to eat. Only she knows how starving is going to help her,' Mrs Kulkarni said looking towards her husband who was quiet.

Again, no one said anything.

'You need to get over this. We know it's difficult but you have to try. You cannot remain like this for rest of your life,' I said trying to avoid any eye contacts.

Again silence followed.

'Get well soon,' I said as I stood up to leave. Few more minutes and I would have started suffocating.

I was having an intense feeling of guilt running through my conscience. But on the other hand, I was trying to surpass it or any other such feeling to interfere with my decision. It was for my betterment. I realised that the centre of my thoughts had shifted from *our* betterment to *my* betterment. But I ignored.

I looked at Kabir signalling him to get up.

'I read your article aunty. It was very bold and appealing,' he said as he stood.

'Yes, it is. But it seems like not everyone admires boldness,' Mr Kulkarni said.

'What happened?' I asked trying to sound like I too have read her article.

The Pragmatic

She signalled that we should not talk about it in Priya's presence. So we walked towards the hall. Mr Kulkarni followed us while Mrs Kulkarni stayed with her.

'What's the issue with the article?' I asked.

'The most obvious one,' he answered.

'Direct reference to Mr Surve's grandson as a culprit,' Kabir said.

'But he is the one, isn't he?' I asked.

'But this hasn't been proved in court yet. So it is not appropriate to claim him as a culprit. We should refer him as a suspect at max. This is what the chief editor of the Newspaper said after he got a phone call from Mr Surve.'

'And what is aunt's response?' Kabir asked.

'She has been asked to write an apology or else she will be fired.'

'Oh God! What will she do know?' I asked.

'She had already sent her resignation letter via a colleague.'

'Resigning for what? Not apologizing? Do they really expect her to apologize to her daughter's rapists?' Kabir asked in an angry voice.

'Yes. They do,' Mr Kulkarni said.

22.

It became quite a news after Mrs Kulkarni's article was published. Mr Surve had given a statement claiming this to be a political game played by oppositions to spoil the reputation of the political party which he formerly led. He added that if his Grandson, Jaykant, was proven to be guilty he will make sure that Jaykant is handed to officers without any trouble.

On the other hand, this situation was creating a pressure on police officers in charge of this case. They were now supposed to find out the truth, which apparently everyone knew, but without Priya's statements was almost impossible to prove. Her doctors were still insisting on not forcing her to recall the catastrophe. But it turned out that doctors were less dominant in deciding what was right for her than people who thought that punishing the criminals will make her feel better. So she was, very politely, forced to speak about what had happened. She couldn't speak about them. As soon as the incident was mentioned she was traumatised and started to speak that they will come back and kidnap her.

This caused further harm to her psychological state and the little improvements she had shown were all ruined. Her condition had become worse after so many attempts to make her talk about the criminals. The frequency of her trauma attacks increased exponentially and this deteriorated her physical condition. New therapists were consulted. All they

The Pragmatic

said was to keep her mind away. To find some distractions so that her focus might shift.

But every now and then some neighbour or some relative will visit her asking about how she felt and how unfortunate she was and similar jibber jabber. Then they would give their expert advice regarding what could be done and which doctors should be consulted and that she must go on a vacation far away from all these. Everyone, apparently being an expert on this subject, gave their unwelcome suggestions unaware of the fact that Kulkarnis were tired of this stuff. Although most people visited her with good intentions, unknowingly, they were making the situation more unbearable for her and for her parents. Finally, Mr Kulkarni grew tired of the things that were making his daughter's life hell and decided to move away. He then withdrew his case so that her daughter had to face no more pressure in conversing with the concerned officials.

Neither did this step proved to be a correct one. This issue had already become a news in the city since the political name was high-lightened. Now withdrawal of the case gave them an opportunity to prove their point. Local newspapers were now filled with the comments made by people, close associates of Mr Surve and his ex-party members, appealing that people should teach their daughters some decency before declaring someone as a criminal and that it's not necessary that it was always a boy who is at fault.

They then declared that Priya was the one who, on her own desire, went in the red light area and requested the people there to make her a part of their world. The story that paper media featured was she is a mentally challenged girl, who, under the fascination of the world of prostitutes, left her home to become one. Later when she was disappointed with her decision she regretted leaving her house.

She shared this with one of her customers, Jaykant Surve, who was ready to help her. Using the advantage of the innocence of this guy, she started claiming that she was kidnapped and made up a story which her parents earlier believed and filed a case against the boy. Now as they realised that it was their daughter who, herself, had ruined her life they have to withdraw the case.

I haven't paid a visit to her place since Mr Kulkarni told about his wife's resignation. Kabir frequently visited her and kept me updated. He had stopped forcing me to come along. In fact, he stopped bothering to ask me whether I will like to join him. I was relieved with this change in his behaviour.

I was worried about what was going to happen to her. I was feeling guilty about not being on her side when she needed me the most. I knew I was not feeling the way I thought I would. I was still attached to her memories and was still stressed and anxious. But some part of me was still holding on to the fact that whatever I was doing was right. All the time we were together, one thing that she always wanted to improve in me was to make my approach towards life more practical. To be a practical person like she was. So here I was, for the first time in my life, making decisions using my brain and not giving a damn to how that makes me feel. Believing that, in the end, I would appreciate my decision.

———

Knock-Knock.

The Pragmatic

It wasn't a typical Kabir's knock. But except Kabir, rarely anyone knocked my door at 1 am. I opened the door and it was Kabir.

'What happened?' I asked. He was crying.

He didn't say anything and entered the room. I closed the door and he sat on my bed rubbing his eyes with his left hand.

I sat next to him, puzzled, placed my arm on his shoulder, 'Kabir, what happened?'

'*Ammi*,' he said referring to his mother, 'she was admitted in ICU.'

'What? I mean why? What happened?' I asked.

'She fell from our terrace,' he said wiping his nose.

'And when did this happen?'

'Last to last week.'

'And she is still in ICU?'

'No.'

'Then?'

'She is out of danger and will be discharged tomorrow. I wasn't informed about any of these.'

'Don't worry she'll be perfectly fine.'

'Yeah, I know. I just want to meet her now and see her for myself.'

'When is the first bus in the morning?' I asked.

'7.30.'

'From?'

'Shivajinagar.'

'So we have to leave from here at around seven' o clock.'

'We? You don't have to come along.'

'Looking at you I doubt you will reach Shivajinagar on your own.'

'But…'

'No buts,' I said, 'go and pack your bags, I will pack mine.' I was ready to go anywhere to escape temporarily from this situation.

Kabir's house was big but spacious is not a word appropriate to describe it. It was completely occupied with furniture and stuff. There was a small temple inside the compound walls. The terrace was recently fenced with brick walls, clearly indicating that they had learnt a lesson from this experience.

His elder brother, Karan, who was also informed yesterday, had reached there an hour before and was upset at his father for hiding this from him. Kabir, on the other hand, was not paying attention to anything but his mother. She was severely injured with six fractured bones, few cracks and a dislocated hip bone. She fell on her right side, first her right hand hitting the ground then her waist and lastly her skull. Thus there was not any serious damage on her skull. This was the reason she survived the accident in spite of having an oversized body.

The Pragmatic

I left the brothers with their mother in her bedroom and came in the hall. Mr Deewan, Kabir's father, was talking, if not begging, with a man who seemed very disappointed and frustrated.

'This is not how we deal in the professional world,' the man said.

'I know. But nothing is hidden from you. You know my reasons and I can't sell my shop now.'

'You have already sold your shop,' he said correcting Mr Deewan.

He was silent.

'I never bother to consider such a request but given your circumstances, I have to accept your request.'

'Thank you, sir.'

'But you have to pay fifty thousand extra.'

'It's too much. Please have some mercy on me.'

'Either pay the extra amount or forget your shop. It's up to you,' the man said.

'Fine. I will pay you the amount till next weekend.'

'Okay,' he shook hands with him and left.

'Arijit, I didn't know you were here,' he said with a smile on his face.

I guess I wasn't supposed to be there. I wanted to ask what was going on but I understood it wasn't the appropriate time to ask.

'I gave them some privacy to have a family talk.'

'You sound like a smart boy. How come you are friends with Kabir,' he said and we both laughed.

'Come inside,' he said signalling me to follow him.

We went to the bedroom again. The mood there was a little less intense now.

'Getting my shop back,' Mr Deewan announced with a broad smile on his face.

I nodded and smiled thinking that this was pleasant news. But none of the two brothers seemed happy to hear this. Mrs Deewan closed her eyes trying to hide her tears. I stopped smiling and tried to remain unnoticeable.

'How much did he add to the original amount?' Sheelu aunty asked.

Sheelu aunty was Mrs Deewan's sister who was there to take care of the patient.

'No. Nothing extra,' he lied.

Apparently, everyone understood that he lied.

———

'Are they sure?' I asked.

'Yes,' Kabir said.

Silence.

He started sobbing heavily. We were sitting in his room and his brother informed him about the reports. Mrs Deewan had lost control over her right leg and will never be able to walk again. His brother left, trying not to cry in front of him.

The Pragmatic

After sobbing for fifteen more minutes Kabir washed his face and came back. His eyes had turn blood red. He sat on the bed stretching his arms wide.

'And that explains why *Abba* was desperate to get his shop back,' he said.

He read the expression of confusion on my face and understood my hesitation to ask anything about his family matters.

'My father owns a stationery shop in the market. The business is quite successful and his shop is very famous in our city.'

'And...' I said when he paused.

'He is working in the shop since he was sixteen when my grandpa died. Being a responsible son he took all the household's responsibilities on his tiny shoulders. Later he got married, we came to his life and his responsibilities and duties never ended. Since I was a kid he used to share his dream of travelling. He frequently mentions his retirement plan of selling his shop and going on long vacations with my mother, who is also fond of travelling, to every corner of India.'

He sighed.

'Now my brother earns well. He looks after my expenses. My father felt it was the right time to retire. So, last month, he sold his shop to a property dealer and was happy thinking about his retirement. *Ammi* told me since he sold his shop all he did was browsing through the brochures of travelling agencies. Both of them share this excitement. They also know that they have little time as they were getting older, they cannot pursue their dream later.'

'And now he got his shop back that means he is not going anywhere,' I said.

'Yeah. Unfortunately.'

―――

After dinner, we all sat in the hall. It was 11 pm and Mrs Deewan and her sister had slept already. We were having a men's talk. One of the wisest discussions in this world. After having few glasses of liquor, apparently, every man becomes wise enough to reveal the way the world is and how life works. Today, this man was Mr Deewan and we were his disciples listening to him and nodding in agreement to whatever he said.

'So how is life my dear boys,' Mr Deewan took the first sip from his third glass of alcohol.

'Great,' I said trying to push away his gaze from me.

'*Abba*, do you think I can take care of *Ammi*?' Karan, Kabir's brother, asked.

'Yes,' Mr Deewan said.

'So can you let her stay with me?'

'Come to the point.'

'*Abba*, sell your shop and go wherever you wish. I am her son. Isn't she equally my responsibility?'

'You think you can take care of her better than me?' Mr Deewan asked in a monotonous voice.

The Pragmatic

'I am not saying that,' Karan said.

'I am sure you are not,' Mr Deewan said.

'Then?'

'What was that girl's name? Tania?'

'No *Abba*. It's Tara,' Karan said.

'Yeah! Tara,' he nodded twice. 'How many times have you told her that you love her?' he asked as he made another glass for himself.

Karan nervously shifted his weight on the couch, 'why are you asking this?'

'Just answer me.'

'Several times.'

'How many times have you seen me telling your mother that I Love her?'

'Never,' Kabir said.

'Not even once,' Karan added.

'Son, when we married I was eighteen and she was sixteen. We spent four decades together sharing our dream of travelling this holy country together. In these four decades, I won't claim I was a good husband. Sometimes I was violent, sometimes drunk evil man and sometimes a moody man driven by lust. She was, on the other hand, a lady living in the boundaries of restrictions bestowed upon on her, first by society and then by her husband. She spent her life living for you and for me. This is the only time when she needs some rest and support. And if I leave her alone, this time, I will not be able to face *almighty*. He will never forgive me. If she can leave behind her family and life when she entered my life shouldn't I reciprocate her sacrifice?

'I never told her that I loved her. But now I have a chance to make her realize that she is far more lovable and important to me than a stupid dream.'

I can see the expression of pride on the faces sitting next to me.

'The only piece of advice I will like to pass to my children is this,' he paused and composed himself, 'never say a woman that you love her unless you mean it. Unless you are ready to reciprocate the sacrifices a woman makes when she changes her last name. Else, just don't say it.

'And if you had already told someone so,' he looked at Karan, 'remember one thing, she is just like your mother. Treat her the way you expect your mother should be treated. No matter what.'

―――

I was again struggling in bed trying to sleep. The conversation with Mr Deewan was replaying in my mind. I never understood this phenomenon of becoming a very different person just after lying in bed. A person who thought a lot, a person who cared a lot about the things I pretended I didn't care about and a person who didn't care about a lot of things I pretended to care about.

To divert my mind I took out the envelope Aryan handed me. While leaving my room I put the envelope in my bag with a thought of reading this on the bus but then Kabir was sitting with me and I didn't want him to know anything about this.

I opened it. It was blue cardboard paper with a rough texture. A letter was written in her beautifully carved handwriting, it read:

Dearest Arijit,

I am not so much good with my words so I am taking help from a book. Here is what I want to say but in a way better manner than I can write. I am giving a book, The Alchemist, along with this letter. The prologue of the book contains the tale of Narcissus. I want you to read the prologue. I want you to understand this is the reason why you are with me and this is the reason I am with you.

Love,
Priya.

22.

'Let me guess,' I said.

'I bet you won't get this one,' Kabir said.

'I guess you are the one standing in the third row and missing the step,' I said pointing towards a little guy in the photograph. The photograph was taken when Kabir was in third grade and had participated in a dance show during the annual gathering of the school.

'No, that isn't me.'

'No. Look carefully he looks totally like you.'

'I think I will know for sure if it's me,' he said.

'Okay-Okay, then which one's you?' I asked.

He took the photograph and pointed towards a thin guy dancing in the front row, 'that's me.'

'You were normal as a kid, weren't you?'

'What do you mean, I am not normal now?'

'I was talking about your size. You were quite slim then.'

'Yeah, I know.'

Meanwhile, his aunt came inside his room bringing two cups of tea. Kabir stood up to take a call and walked out of the room.

The Pragmatic

'I never understood how personal your phone calls are. Why always you have to skip away from elders to take calls?' she asked.

'Maybe he didn't want to take that call in front of me.'

'Do I look that stupid to you?' she asked.

'No, I was just trying to defend my friend,' I said smiling.

'Well tried,' she said and left the room.

I took a sip of tea from the cup and felt the warm gulp of tea passing through my food-pipe. I remembered my cigarette puff. I flipped through few more photographs in the album till Kabir arrived.

He came inside and locked the door. As he turned I looked at his face and sensed that something terrible had happened.

'What's the matter?' I asked.

He sat on the bed without saying anything and started to wipe his eyes.

'Who was on the call?'

'Priya's dad,' he said not looking at me.

That wasn't something I wanted to hear.

'What did he say?' I asked.

'Nothing,' he said.

'Just tell me,' I said.

'It's about Priya.'

'What happened Kabir?'

'She attempted suicide.'

'And?'

He sighed, 'and she succeeded.'

After a couple of minutes of painful silence, Kabir stood up and unlocked the door.

'Don't speak with anyone about this. People here are already in enough pain,' he said. 'I'll be back after washing my face.'

And he left. I looked away at the window.

I wondered whether things would have been different if I haven't chosen the path I did. I knew that nothing was going to make any difference but I didn't want to feel guilty about it rest of the time. So I was trying to convince myself that whatever I did was the right thing. But no matter how much one tries, one cannot convince anyone including and especially our own self to believe in something which we don't actually believe in.

I realised I haven't done the right thing. Although I didn't know how much I mattered in her life in the given scenario. I still knew that I could have been a better person, at least a better friend than I proved to be.

Now whatever remains for me is regret, crying, sobbing and being ashamed of my selfishness. This selfishness is what I tried to cover in the name of being practical.

Probably Kabir was right, probably Sarang was wrong, probably I never understood what he tried to say.

But after this, I was helpless as there was nothing I could've done. In the time when I could've done something, I did nothing besides making things worse for her.

The door opened and Kabir came inside with a fresh face.

'You think we should leave?' I asked, 'if you want to stay you may, but I want to return.'

'Arijit,' he said smiling.

'What?' his smile made me worry. Why was he smiling? After I came to know about his mental illness I was unnecessarily worrying certain times. This was one such moment.

'You know John Lennon?' he asked.

'Why are you asking this now?'

'Just answer.'

'No.'

'Okay, he once said, "Everything will be okay in the end. If it's not okay, it's not the end," sounds great, doesn't it?'

'Are you talking to me?'

'Yes, Arijit I am talking to you.'

'Come to the point.'

'Sure. It is said that *it's always easy to be wise after the event.* You, too, might have realised what you should have done as there's nothing you think you can do now.'

'I am getting where this conversation is headed. Yes, you were right, happy?'

'No, you are no getting. I'll tell you in a minute but before tell me whether you think what you did was appropriate?'

'How does it matter Kabir? What do you want? To know that you were right and I was wrong. Well then yes you were right. And let's just stop here, shall we?'

He was smiling now. And I was getting mad because given all the conditions, he was happy just because he was right.

'Arijit, it wasn't a call from Priya's father.'

I gave him a blank look.

'I tried something on you and now I see that it worked, actually I was scared if it won't you'd kill me.'

I was still quiet and tried to comprehend the situation.

'You know you should be in a mental hospital?' I asked.

'Yes I know,' he said smiling.

'No I mean it, you son of a bitch, you rascal, you bastard.'

He was still smiling.

After abusing him, shouting on him that he scared the hell out me and becoming red hot with anger, I finally calmed down and realised that he was indeed a genius in doing what he did. But I didn't say this in front of him. I was mad at him and he, in return, was calm and smiling. Which made me angrier.

I was back on track and now that I've realised my mistake I was feeling terrible about myself. The difference between a right and a wrong decision is simply the way you feel afterwards. Now, after so many days, I was feeling that the heavy stone has been lifted off my chest.

Anyway, the realisation of the problem was the first half and whatever was remaining was the second half.

———

'Just say sorry,' Kabir said. Lights were turned off and the room was completely dark. Kabir was sleeping next to me on his bed.

'No that's not an option.'

'Why?'

'She'll say *it's okay*, without actually meaning it. And I will be left without anything to say in a terrible position,' I said.

'So?'

'I don't know.'

I sighed.

'How could I be so selfish? So blindfolded?' I don't think I can face her now.'

'Calm down Arijit, take a deep breath and relax.'

'You know you're not helping in any way.'

'I know but this is the best I can say.'

'Okay, so here I am discussing how to face a girl whom I left when she most needed me, and all you can come up is to take a deep breath?'

'You know what, don't say anything. Let's just meet her and pretend that everything is normal. This has always worked for me.'

I didn't respond to what he said.

'Or rather I'll keep quiet, this might be more helpful,' he said and that was quite appropriate.

'She is having far bigger problems to deal with and her psychological state is getting worse. I don't want to be sympathetic to her neither do I want to look like I am feeling sympathy for her and which is why I want to be at her side.'

'Hmm,' Kabir said.

'And why am I talking about this to you?'

'I don't know, but you may carry on if you want.'

'I would rather try to sleep,' I said and buried my face in the cushion.

'Arijit,' Kabir said after five minutes, 'have you slept?'

'Yes,' I said.

'Then how are you answering me?'

'I am talking in my dreams.'

'Shut up and listen,' he was still talking from under his blanket.

'What?'

———

'You've become a clinomaniac, haven't you?' I asked.

'What's clinomaniaic?' Kabir asked.

'Strong desire to remain in bed,' I said.

'Oh, like suffering from that disease called dysania?' Kabir asked.

'For god's sake, Dysania is not a disease. It' a state of mind,' I said.

'Whatever, Priya told us it's a disease, remember?'

'No, she didn't.'

'She did.'

'Arijit is right,' Priya said, 'It's not a disease.'

Since an hour we were trying to make her talk but all she said was either yes or no. And now finally she was up to something. Two months have passed since I returned from Kabir's hometown.

'And clinomania is synonymous with Dysania,' she added.

'Look, I was right,' I said trying to pretend that her participation in our conversation was perfectly normal.

'Where did you learn that?' she asked.

'Learned what?'

'That word.'

'What do you think only you are the one who can use big words? I too am sesquipedalianist.'

'Impressive,' she said, 'now shut up and tell me from where you are learning this words.'

'There is a new app which presents an interesting word, sometimes not officially in use, and its meaning every day,' I said.

'And what does sis-queue whatever you said means?'

'A person who uses long words, sometimes unnecessarily,' she said.

'Is there any word like anti-ses-queue whatever? I would love to get a t-shirt printed with that word,' Kabir said.

'Okay now check out this word, I bet you don't know it's meaning,' I said.

'Bring it on,' she said.

'*Benkinersophobia.*'

'Fear of not receiving a letter from Hogwarts School of Witchcraft and Wizardry on one's eleventh birthday,' she said in a mechanical tone.

'What about this- *Petrichor*.'

'The scent of rain after dust,' she said.

'Let me play my Ace of Spades-*Selenophile*?'

'I don't know what it means but it is quite easy to deduce. *Selena* is Moon goddess and *Phile* is for love or fondness; so I'll go with - Love for the moon.'

'Damn it, I don't want to play,' I said.

She smiled, 'am I right?'

The Pragmatic

'Hell you are,' I said.

'Let me ask you one,' she said. 'But this one isn't English, it's a Latin word- *Tacenda*.'

Obviously, I didn't know the answer.

'How am I supposed to know the meaning of a Latin word?'

'Well, you're not supposed to know, you're supposed to find out the meaning of this word,' she said and lifted herself sitting straight on the bed.

'I'll try,' I said, '*Tacenda*.'

ABOUT THE AUTHOR

    Yogesh Pandey, 21, is currently pursuing his post graduate degree from Fergusson College, Pune.
    He is an avid reader, a freelance writer and an indigenously humorous and jovial guy.
    The Pragmatic is his debut novel.
    Yogesh can be reached at authoryogesh@yahoo.com

www.ingramcontent.com/pod-product-compliance
Lightning Source LLC
Chambersburg PA
CBHW022114040426
42450CB00006B/696